111 Onion Soup Recipes

(111 Onion Soup Recipes - Volume 1)

Judy Gordy

Copyright: Published in the United States by Judy Gordy/ © JUDY GORDY

Published on November, 24 2020

All rights reserved. No part of this publication may be reproduced, stored in retrieval system, copied in any form or by any means, electronic, mechanical, photocopying, recording or otherwise transmitted without written permission from the publisher. Please do not participate in or encourage piracy of this material in any way. You must not circulate this book in any format. JUDY GORDY does not control or direct users' actions and is not responsible for the information or content shared, harm and/or actions of the book readers.

In accordance with the U.S. Copyright Act of 1976, the scanning, uploading and electronic sharing of any part of this book without the permission of the publisher constitute unlawful piracy and theft of the author's intellectual property. If you would like to use material from the book (other than just simply for reviewing the book), prior permission must be obtained by contacting the author at author@limerecipes.com

Thank you for your support of the author's rights.

Content

CHAPTER 1: FRENCH ONION SOUP RECIPES 5

1. Baked French Onion Soup Recipe 5
2. Baked White Wine & Onion Soup Recipe . 5
3. Classic Fall French Onion Soup Recipe 6
4. Classic French Onion Soup Recipe 7
5. Crock Pot French Onion Soup Recipe 7
6. Crockpot French Onion Soup With Cheesy Bread Recipe 8
7. Easy Creamy Onion Soup Recipe 8
8. Easy French Onion Soup Recipe 9
9. Easy Onion Soup Recipe 9
10. Extraordinary French Onion Soup Recipe . 9
11. FRENCH ONION SOUP 10
12. FRENCH ONION SOUP Recipe 10
13. French Chicken Onion Soup With Cheese Toast Recipe 11
14. French Garlic Onion Soup Recipe 11
15. French Onion Soup 1 Recipe 12
16. French Onion Soup Gratinee Recipe 12
17. French Onion Soup Modified From Sandra Lee Recipe 13
18. French Onion Soup Recipe 14
19. French Roasted Onion Soup With Thyme Recipe 14
20. Golden French Onion Soup Recipe 14
21. Guinness French Onion Soup Recipe 15
22. Hearty French Onion Soup Recipe 16
23. Julia Child French Onion Soup Recipe 16
24. Julia Childs French Onion Soup Grantineed With Cheese Recipe 17
25. Mediterranean Style French Onion Soup Recipe 17
26. Mellissa D'arabian's French Onion Soup Recipe 18
27. Onion Soup With Champagne Recipe 18
28. Paula Deens French Onion Soup Recipe . 19
29. Rather French Onion Soup Recipe 19
30. Simple French Onion Soup Recipe 20
31. Super Easy French Onion Soup Recipe 20
32. Tomato French Onion Soup Recipe 21
33. Tyler Florences French Onion Soup Recipe 21
34. Vegetarian French Onion Recipe 22
35. Vegetarian French Onion Soup Recipe 22
36. French Onion Soup Recipe 22

CHAPTER 2: AWESOME ONION SOUP RECIPES 23

37. Angel Hair And Three Onion Soup Recipe 23
38. Asparagus Soup Puree With Green Onion Recipe 23
39. Aztec Onion And Lime Soup With Blue Corn Dumplings Recipe 24
40. Baked Onion Soup Recipe 25
41. Banana And Onion Soup Recipe 25
42. Beef Jerky And Onion Soup Recipe 25
43. Beef And Onion Stew Stifado Recipe 26
44. Beer, Onion And Carrot Soup Recipe 26
45. Bennigans Onion Soup Copycat Recipe ... 27
46. Booming Onion Rhubarb Soup Recipe 27
47. Buttermilk Bisque With Cucumbers And Onions Recipe 27
48. Cams Onion Soup Recipe 28
49. Canadian Onion Soup Recipe 28
50. Cantaloupe Honeydew And Sweet Onion Gazpacho With Crispy Prosciutto Recipe 29
51. Caramelized Onion Portobello Mushroom Soup With Goat Cheese Croutons Recipe 29
52. Caramelized Onion And Parmesan Cheese Soup Recipe 30
53. Carbonnade A La Flamande Belgian Beef Beer And Onion Stew Recipe 30
54. Carmelized Onion Shitake Soup With Gruyere Blue Cheese Toasts Recipe 31
55. Carrot Onion Soup With A Toasted Cashew Garnish Recipe 32
56. Chicken Onion Soup Recipe 32
57. Cream Of Onion Soup Recipe 33
58. Cream Of Vidalia Onion Soup Recipe 33
59. Creamy Curry Onion Soup Recipe 34
60. Creamy Onion Soup Recipe 34
61. Curried Pumpkin Soup With Maple Caramelized Onions Recipe 35
62. Curried Pumpkin Soup With Mushrooms And Onions Recipe 35
63. Delicate Clear Onion Soup Recipe 36
64. English Onion Soup With Sage And Chedder Recipe 36

65. First Place Award Winning Onion Soup Recipe 37
66. Five Onion Soup With Garlic Croutons Recipe 37
67. French Onion Soup 38
68. French Onion Soup Gratinee Recipe 38
69. Garlicky Onion Soup Recipe 39
70. Golden Onion Soup Recipe 39
71. Greek Onion Stew Stefado Recipe 40
72. Krums Vidalia Onion Soup Recipe 41
73. Kumera And Cumin Soup With Carmalised Onions Recipe 41
74. Lovely Healthy N Yummy Butternut Squash Soup With Caramelized Onions And Apples Recipe 42
75. Mexican Red Onion Soup Recipe 42
76. Onion And Pepper Soup Recipe 43
77. Onion Chowder Recipe 43
78. Onion Ham And Cheese Chowder Recipe 43
79. Onion Rivel Soup Recipe 44
80. Onion Soup Mix Recipe............................ 44
81. Onion Soup Recipe 44
82. Onion Soup With A British Twist Recipe 45
83. Onion Soup In English Recipe.................. 45
84. Onion Wine Soup Recipe 46
85. Onion And Chorizo Soup Recipe 46
86. Onion And Garlic Soup Recipe................. 46
87. Onion Soup Recipe 47
88. Outback Steakhouse Walkabout Onion Soup Recipe 47
89. Philly Cheese Steak Onion Soup For 2 Recipe 48
90. Pork With Eggplants Peppers And Spring Onions Recipe 48
91. Potato And Onion Soup Recipe................ 49
92. Potato Onion Cheddar Soup Recipe 49
93. Potato Onion Soup With Pesto Recipe..... 50
94. Potato And Onion Soup Recipe................ 50
95. ROASTED ONION SOUP Recipe 50
96. Red Onion And Blue Cheese Soup Recipe 51
97. Rich Two Onion And Garlic Soup Recipe 51
98. Roasted Pumpkin And Onion Bisque Recipe 51
99. Roaster Onion Soup Recipe 52
100. Rosy Onion Soup Recipe 52
101. Simple Red Onion Soup Recipe 53
102. Slow Roasted Onion Soup Recipe.......... 53
103. Smoked Eggplant Onion And Apple Soup Recipe 54
104. Smoked Onion And Garlic Soup Recipe .. 54
105. Sweet Potato And Onion Soup Recipe 55
106. The Soup Of Many Onions Recipe............ 55
107. Triple Onion And Potato Soup Recipe 56
108. Tuscan Onion Soup With Shaved Parmesan Recipe 56
109. Uber Allium Soup Recipe 57
110. Vidalia Onion Soup Recipe.................... 57
111. Golden Onion Soup Recipe 58

INDEX 59
CONCLUSION 61

Chapter 1: French Onion Soup Recipes

***

1. Baked French Onion Soup Recipe

Serving: 8 | Prep: | Cook: 40mins | Ready in:

Ingredients

- 6 large white onions, thinly sliced
- 3 cloves garlic, finely minced
- 2 tablespoons olive oil
- 2 tablespoons butter
- 9 cups beef broth or homemade stock
- 1/4 cup of dry red drinking wine (optional)
- 1/4 teaspoon onion powder
- 1/3 teaspoon ground black pepper
- salt to taste
- 8 large croutons, buttered and baked-- plus extra bread for dunking
- 1 cup shredded parmesan cheese
- 8 large slices gruyere cheese
- Serve with an AUTUMN SUNSET cocktail

Direction

- Preheat oven to 325°F. Bake bread pieces 15 to 20 minutes or until lightly golden and crisped. Set aside.
- Sauté sliced onions in olive oil and butter over medium heat until onions become translucent but not brown. Add minced garlic cloves to onions during last few minutes, making sure garlic does not brown.
- Stir in beef broth, wine and seasonings.
- Bring to a boil; reduce, heat and simmer for 30 to 40 minutes. Adjust seasonings to taste adding salt and pepper as required. Remember that Parmesan cheese is salty, so don't overdo with the salt.
- Ladle the soup into ovenproof serving bowls, one for each serving. Cover soup with a slice of bread. Top with Gruyere and sprinkle with Parmesan.
- Place serving bowls under broiler set on high. Broil six to seven minutes or until cheese is bubbly and has some browning.
- Serve with additional grated Parmesan cheese for sprinkling at table.

2. Baked White Wine & Onion Soup Recipe

Serving: 4 | Prep: | Cook: 2hours | Ready in:

Ingredients

- 2 tbsp butter
- 4 to 5 medium onions, thinly sliced
- 1/2 cup dry white wine
- 4 cups vegetable stock (you can use chicken)
- 1 bay leaf
- 1/4 tsp thyme
- 1/4 tsp marjoram
- 4 rounds toasted French bread
- 1 cup grated gruyere cheese
- salt & pepper to taste

Direction

- Melt butter in large deep skillet. When hot, add onions and cook, uncovered, 30 minutes over medium low heat. Stir a few times during cooking.
- Pour in wine & mix well. Cook over medium heat until wine reduces to half. (About 3-4 minutes)
- Pour in stock, mix well, add bay leaf and all seasonings. Mix well and cook, uncovered, about 35 minutes over low heat.
- Preheat oven to 425 degrees.

- Ladle soup into individual ovenproof onion soup bowls. Cover with toasted rounds, top with grated Gruyere. Bake about 15 minutes or until cheese is bubbly brown.

3. Classic Fall French Onion Soup Recipe

Serving: 0 | Prep: | Cook: 60mins | Ready in:

Ingredients

- INGREDIENTS:
- 1/4 cup unsalted butter
- 3 pounds (about 5 medium) sweet onions, sliced
- 2 cloves garlic, minced
- 1/2 Bottle of Red Wine
- 6 cups beef stock
- 4 sprigs fresh thyme
- 2 bay leaves
- 2 teaspoons white wine vinegar
- Kosher salt and freshly ground black pepper, to taste
- 12 (3/4-inch-thick) French baguette slices
- 1 cup shredded Swiss cheese
- 1 cup shredded Gruyere cheese
- DIRECTIONS:
- Melt butter in a large stockpot or Dutch oven over medium heat. Add onions, and cook, stirring often, until deep golden brown and caramelized, about 30-40 minutes.* Stir in garlic until fragrant, about 1 minute.
- Stir in wine, scraping any browned bits from the bottom of the stockpot.
- Stir in beef stock, thyme and bay leaves. Bring to a boil; reduce heat and simmer, stirring occasionally, until slightly reduced, about 15-20 minutes. Remove and discard thyme sprigs and bay leaves.
- Stir in white wine vinegar; season with salt and pepper, to taste.
- Preheat oven to broil.
- Place baguette slices onto a baking sheet. Place into oven and broil until golden brown on both sides, about 1-2 minutes per side; set aside.
- Divide soup into ramekins or ovenproof bowls. Place onto a baking sheet. Top with baguette slices to cover the surface of the soup completely; sprinkle with cheeses. Place into oven and broil until golden brown and cheeses have melted; about 2 minutes.
- Serve immediately.
- NOTES:
- *If the onions begin to burn on the bottom of the pot, reduce heat slightly and stir in 1/4 cup water.

Direction

- Melt butter in a large stockpot or Dutch oven over medium heat. Add onions, and cook, stirring often, until deep golden brown and caramelized, about 30-40 minutes.* Stir in garlic until fragrant, about 1 minute.
- Stir in wine, scraping any browned bits from the bottom of the stockpot.
- Stir in beef stock, thyme and bay leaves. Bring to a boil; reduce heat and simmer, stirring occasionally, until slightly reduced, about 15-20 minutes. Remove and discard thyme sprigs and bay leaves.
- Stir in white wine vinegar; season with salt and pepper, to taste.
- Preheat oven to broil.
- Place baguette slices onto a baking sheet. Place into oven and broil until golden brown on both sides, about 1-2 minutes per side; set aside.
- Divide soup into ramekins or ovenproof bowls. Place onto a baking sheet. Top with baguette slices to cover the surface of the soup completely; sprinkle with cheeses. Place into oven and broil until golden brown and cheeses have melted; about 2 minutes.
- Serve immediately.
- NOTES:

- *If the onions begin to burn on the bottom of the pot, reduce heat slightly and stir in 1/4 cup water.

4. Classic French Onion Soup Recipe

Serving: 4 | Prep: | Cook: 90mins | Ready in:

Ingredients

- 4 tablespoons unsalted butter
- 2 pounds (2 or 3 large) yellow onions, sliced ¼" thick
- 1 ½ teaspoons granulated sugar
- 1 tablespoon all-purpose flour
- ¾ cup dry red wine
- 3 ½ cups Homemade beef or veal stock
- 2 teaspoons chopped fresh thyme
- salt and freshly ground black pepper
- 1 small baguette, sliced into ½-inch pieces
- 1 ½ cups grated regular Gruyère
- 1 ½ cups grated smoked Gruyère

Direction

- Melt butter in a large Dutch oven on medium - medium-low heat.
- Add onions, spreading them out in as thin a layer as possible.
- Sprinkle with sugar, and cook, stirring just as needed to keep onions from sticking, until they are soft, golden brown, and just starting to caramelize - about 1 hour.
- Sprinkle flour over onions, and stir to coat.
- Cook flour for about 5 minutes. Add wine, stock, and thyme, and bring to a simmer.
- Cook, partially covered, for about 30 minutes, to allow the flavours to combine.
- Season with salt and pepper to taste.
- Meanwhile, lightly toast at least 8 slices of bread under a broiler or in the toaster and set aside.
- Ladle hot soup into four ovenproof bowls and arrange on a sturdy baking sheet.
- Place 2 -3 slices (depending on size) of toasted bread over each bowl of soup.
- Mix together the two grated cheeses and sprinkle ¾ cup over bread in each bowl.
- Place soup bowls under the broiler until cheese is melted and crusty brown around the edges.
- Watch carefully that bread doesn't burn.
- Serve immediately.
- I find this soup to be both rustic and elegant...easy to make and delicious to indulge in.

5. Crock Pot French Onion Soup Recipe

Serving: 8 | Prep: | Cook: 40mins | Ready in:

Ingredients

- Soup
- 3 large onions, slice
- 3 Tbl butter, melted
- 3 Tbl flour
- 1 Tbl worcestershire sauce
- 1 tsp sugar
- 1/4 tsp pepper
- 4 14 1/2 ounce cans oc beef broth
- (1/4 cup red wine, brandy or ale can be added as well)
- Cheesy Broiled French bread
- 8 slices French bread 1 inch thick
- 3/4 C shredded mozzarella
- 2 Tbl shredded or grated Parmesan

Direction

- Mix onions and butter in a 3 1/2 to 6 qt. slow cooker
- Cover and cook on high1 to 3 hours or until onions begin to brown slightly around the edges (it depends on your crock pot)
- Whisk flour, Worcestershire, sugar and pepper
- Stir flour mixture and broth into onions

- Cover and cook on low heat 7 to 9 hours or until onions are very tender
- Make Cheesy Broiled Bread and place 1 slice on each bowl of soup
- Set oven to broil
- Place bread slices on rack in broiler pan
- Sprinkle with cheeses
- Broil about 5 to 6 ' from heat about 3 minutes or until cheese is melted

- Cover: cook on low for 7-9 hours or high for 3-4 hours
- About 10 minutes before serving, place bread on a broiler pan and sprinkle with the mozza and parmesan cheese
- (I may try next time to put the bread and soup in the oven under broil for more flavour)
- Broil until the cheese is bubbly
- Top individual servings of soup with 1 slice and serve

6. Crockpot French Onion Soup With Cheesy Bread Recipe

Serving: 6 | Prep: | Cook: 12mins | Ready in:

Ingredients

- 3 large onions, sliced then havled (about 3 cups)
- 3 tbsp margarine, melted
- 1 tsp sugar
- 1/4 pepper (or how much you would like)
- 1 tbsp worchestershire sauce
- 4 (14oz) cans of beef broth
- 8 (1 inch thick) slices of French bread
- 3 oz (3/4 cup) shredded mozza cheese (I bet swiss would be nice) I just added enough cheese to my likeing
- 2 tbsp parmesan cheese
- *** I cut this recipe in half to serve 2-3 people***

Direction

- In your slow cooker, add the onions and the melted margarine
- Cover and cook on high for 30-35 minutes until the onions get a little brown around the edges
- In a small bowl. Blend the flour, sugar, pepper and Worcestershire sauce and a little bit of broth until it forms a paste (or close to it)
- Stir the flour mixture and broth into the crockpot with onions

7. Easy Creamy Onion Soup Recipe

Serving: 8 | Prep: | Cook: 20mins | Ready in:

Ingredients

- 9 tablespoons flour
- 9 tablespoons butter + 1
- 3 cups of milk
- 1 can of chicken broth
- 2 cans of French onion soup
- 1 onion
- 1 tablespoon sugar
- 1 teaspoon coarse salt

Direction

- Chop onion and sauté in 1 tablespoon butter, salt, and sugar, set aside.
- Make a white sauce with butter, flour, and milk. (Melt butter, slowly whisk in flour, slowly whisk in milk.)
- Add French onion soup, chicken broth, and onions, and heat on low to medium (depending on your stove top, just heat till desired temperature) for ten minutes and serve.

8. Easy French Onion Soup Recipe

Serving: 8 | Prep: | Cook: 75mins | Ready in:

Ingredients

- 3 pounds onions, thinly sliced - use the slicer on the food processor!
- 6 16 ounce cans beef broth (or chicken or a combination
- 6 cans water
- 1 stick butter
- 1 teaspoon thyme
- salt and pepper, to taste
- 1/4 c. sherry - optional
- shredded swiss cheese
- parmesan cheese

Direction

- Sauté onions in butter until soft but not brown. Add broth, water, thyme, salt & pepper. Simmer about an hour and 15 minutes. Before serving you can add 1/4 cup sherry.
- Ladle soup into oven proof bowls & float a thick, toasted slice of French bread on top of soup. Quickly layer shredded Swiss cheese & dust with parmesan then another layer of Swiss and bake soup at 425 until puffed & brown.
- Leftover soup may be frozen...without the bread and cheese, of course.

9. Easy Onion Soup Recipe

Serving: 8 | Prep: | Cook: 30mins | Ready in:

Ingredients

- 2 LARGE shallots
- 1 LARGE red onion
- I LARGE white onion
- 1 BOTTLE red wine
- TBS. butter ROOM TEMP

Direction

- Chop or slice all onions, cooks choice
- In a large pan or wok pour in red wine and simmer on low heat, also add all onions
- Bring to simmer, taste, the alcohol should be evaporated, then whisk in butter
- You can top with shredded gruyere cheese, croutons, or cheese bread sticks
- 3, 16 oz. cans of dark beer, I use Yuengling, can replace red wine, just cook out the alcohol, with the beer shredded gruyere is really good as soon as it's in the bowls,
- Gruyere melts fast

10. Extraordinary French Onion Soup Recipe

Serving: 4 | Prep: | Cook: 50mins | Ready in:

Ingredients

- 4 slices French bread
- 2 tablespoons butter
- 3 medium onions thinly sliced
- 1 clove garlic mined
- 1/4 teaspoon sugar
- 1/4 cup dry white wine
- 2 tablespoons flour
- 1 bay leaf
- 4 cups beef broth
- 2 cups water
- 1 teaspoon salt
- 1 teaspoon freshly ground black pepper
- 1 cup grated gruyere cheese
- Grated parmesan cheese

Direction

- Toast bread in 350 oven for 15 minutes. In a large heavy saucepan melt butter over medium heat until it begins to foam. Reduce heat to low and add onions and garlic then simmer uncovered for 15 minutes stirring occasionally, adding butter during cooking process if necessary. Increase heat to medium then add sugar and sauté for 30 minutes. Increase heat to high then pour the wine into the onions and reduce the liquid by 2/3. Reduce heat to medium and sprinkle flour onto the onions and stir until all traces of flour disappear. Gradually stir in broth and water then add bay leaf and season with salt and pepper. Bring to boil then reduce heat and simmer uncovered for 30 minutes stirring occasionally. Remove bay leaf then pour hot soup into bowls and float bread on top. Sprinkle generously with gruyere cheese and a little grated parmesan. Broil soup in the middle of the oven for 20 minutes.

11. FRENCH ONION SOUP

Serving: 0 | Prep: | Cook: | Ready in:

Ingredients

- 4 pounds yellow onions, peeled and thinly sliced (approximately 5–6 large onions)
- 3 tablespoons butter
- 4 cloves garlic, minced
- 3 tablespoons flour
- 1/2 cup dry white wine
- 6 cups of beef stock (or veggie stock)
- 1 teaspoon Worcestershire sauce
- 1 bay leaf
- 3 sprigs fresh thyme (or 1 teaspoon dried thyme)
- fine sea salt and freshly-cracked black pepper, to taste
- baguette
- grated or sliced cheese (such as Gruyere, Asiago, Swiss, Gouda or Mozzarella)

Direction

- Caramelize the onions. In a large heavy-bottomed stockpot, melt the butter over medium-high heat. Add the onions and sauté until well for about 30 minutes until caramelized (but not burnt), initially stirring every 3-5 minutes, then about once a minute near the end of caramelization to prevent burning*. Add garlic and sauté for 2 minutes. Stir in the flour and cook for an additional 1 minute. Stir in the wine to deglaze the pan, using a wooden spoon to scrape up any browned bits on the bottom of the pan.
- Simmer the soup. Add the stock, Worcestershire, bay leaf, and thyme and stir to combine. Continue to cook until the soup reaches a simmer. Then reduce heat to medium-low, cover and simmer for at least 10 minutes. Discard the bay leaf and sprigs of thyme. Taste the soup and season with salt and pepper as needed.
- Toast the bread. Preheat oven to 400°F. While the soup is simmering, slice the baguette into 1-inch thick pieces and arrange them in single layer on baking sheet. Bake for 6-8 minutes, until the bread is toasted and golden around the edges. Remove and set aside.
- Broil the topping. Switch the oven to the broiler. Once the soup is ready to serve, place your oven-safe bowls on a thick baking sheet. Ladle the soup into each bowl, then top with a baguette slice and your desired amount of cheese (I used about 1/4 cup shredded cheese for each). Place on an oven rack about 6 inches from the heat and broil for 2-4 minutes, or until the cheese is melted and bubbly. (Keep a close eye on them so that they do not burn.) Remove from the oven and serve immediately while the soup is hot and bubbly.

12. FRENCH ONION SOUP Recipe

Serving: 6 | Prep: | Cook: 90mins | Ready in:

Ingredients

- 3 lbs onions peeled and sliced
- 2 cloves of garlic peeled and finely minced
- 4 oz unsalted butter

- 1 tablespoon olive oil
- 2 bay leaves and 2 sprigs thyme tied together
- 3 1/4 pints fresh beef stock
- 1 teaspoon brandy
- 2 glasses white wine
- 1 baquette sliced at an angle
- 8-10 oz grated gruyere cheese
- fresh gorund baclk pepper
- 1 teaspoon sea salt

Direction

- Heat butter and olive in saucepan with heavy bottom. When melted add onions, pepper, salt and bay leaf and thyme, stir. Gently cook over low heat for about 20 minutes, stir every few minutes order avoid onions getting burnt. Uncover add garlic and brandy and cook for 20-30 mins stirring frequently till caramelized
- Stir in flour and stir very frequently in order avoid flour gets lumpy and cook for further 3 minutes till mixed thoroughly with onions
- Pour wine and stock, bring to boil...and simmer for 25 minutes.
- Remove bay leaf and thyme sprigs.
- Toast the baguette slices. Put a heap of cheese on top of each and place a centre of dish and ladle the hot and heart soup on top
- And that's it......................bon appetit

13. French Chicken Onion Soup With Cheese Toast Recipe

Serving: 8 | Prep: | Cook: 45mins | Ready in:

Ingredients

- 2 12.5 oz cans boneless chicken breast
- 2 T butter
- 5 large onions (2 lbs) cut into thin half moons
- 2 T flour
- 2 14.5 oz cans beef broth
- 2 14.5 oz cans chicken broth
- 1 c dry white wine
- salt & ground pepper to taste
- 8 slices of French or Italian bread
- 1 c shredded Swiss or gruyere cheese

Direction

- Melt butter in a large saucepan.
- Add onions and reduce the heat to medium-low.
- Cover and cook, stirring occasionally, until the onions are tender, about 30 minutes.
- Uncover and increase the heat to medium-high.
- Cook, stirring often, until the onions are golden brown, about 5 minutes.
- Add the flour and stir to cook the flour, about 1 minute.
- Pour in the broths and the wine.
- Bring to a simmer, scraping up the browned bits on the bottom of the pan.
- Add the chicken meat to the soup and season to taste with the salt and pepper.
- When ready to serve, position the broiler rack about 6 inches from the source of the heat and preheat the broiler.
- Broil the bread slices until lightly toasted.
- Turn the bread over and mound the cheese on each slice.
- Broil until the cheese is bubbling, about 2 minutes.
- Serve the soup hot, floating a cheese toast on each serving.

14. French Garlic Onion Soup Recipe

Serving: 4 | Prep: | Cook: 30mins | Ready in:

Ingredients

- 1 whole head of garlic
- olive oil
- 1 sweet onion
- 4 c water
- 3 tsp beef bouillon
- salt and pepper to taste

- pepper jack cheese
- crusty French bread

Direction

- Slice garlic and onions into thin strips.
- Heat oil in a pot.
- Add garlic and onion.
- Cook till translucent.
- Add water and bouillon.
- Simmer about 20 minutes.
- Serve in a bowl with a slice of bread and cheese to top.

15. French Onion Soup 1 Recipe

Serving: 46 | Prep: | Cook: 50mins | Ready in:

Ingredients

- French onion soup
- 1/2 cup unsalted butter
- 4 onions, sliced
- 2 garlic cloves, chopped
- 2 bay leaves
- 2 fresh thyme sprigs
- kosher salt and freshly ground black pepper
- 1 cup red wine
- 3 heaping tablespoons all-purpose flour
- 2 quarts beef broth
- 1 baguette, sliced
- 1/2 pound grated gruyere

Direction

- Melt the stick of butter in a large pot over medium heat. Add the onions, garlic, bay leaves, thyme, and salt and pepper and cook until the onions are very soft and caramelized, about 25 minutes. Add the wine, bring to a boil, reduce the heat and simmer until the wine has evaporated and the onions are dry, about 5 minutes. Discard the bay leaves and thyme sprigs. Dust the onions with the flour and give them a stir. Turn the heat down to medium low so the flour doesn't burn, and cook for 10 minutes to cook out the raw flour taste. Now add the beef broth, bring the soup back to a simmer, and cook for 10 minutes. Season, to taste, with salt and pepper.
- When you're ready to eat, preheat the broiler. Arrange the baguette slices on a baking sheet in a single layer. Sprinkle the slices with the Gruyere and broil until bubbly and golden brown, 3 to 5 minutes.
- Ladle the soup in bowls and float several of the Gruyere croutons on top.
- Alternative method: Ladle the soup into bowls, top each with 2 slices of bread and top with cheese. Put the bowls into the oven to toast the bread and melt the cheese.

16. French Onion Soup Gratinee Recipe

Serving: 24 | Prep: | Cook: 45mins | Ready in:

Ingredients

- 4 oz butter
- 5 lb onion sliced thin
- 6.5 qt beef stock, or half beef and half chicken stock
- salt and pepper to taste
- 5 fl oz Sherry 4-6 fl oz, optional
- as needed, each:
- French bread (see directions)
- 1.5 lb Gruyère or swiss cheese, or a mixture, coarsely grated

Direction

- Heat the butter in a stockpot over moderate heat.
- Add the onions and cook until they are golden.
- Stir occasionally.
- Note:
- The onions must cook slowly and become evenly browned.

- This is a slow process and will take about 30 minutes.
- Do not brown too fast or use high heat.
- Add the stock and bring to a boil.
- Simmer until the onions are very tender and the flavours are well blended, about 20 minutes.
- Season to taste with salt and pepper.
- Add the sherry, if desired.
- Cut the bread into slices about .38 in thick.
- You will need 1 or 2 slices per portion, or just enough to cover the top of the soup in its serving crock.
- Toast the slices in the oven or under the broiler.
- For each portion fill an individual service soup crock with hot soup.
- Place 1 or 2 slices of the toast on top and cover with cheese.
- Pass under the broiler until the cheese is bubbling and lightly browned.
- Serve immediately.
- Note:
- Onion soup may be served without gratinéeing and with cheese croutons prepared separately.
- Toast the bread as in basic recipe.
- Place on a sheet pan.
- Brush lightly with butter and sprinkle each piece with grated cheese.
- (Parmesan may be mixed with the other cheese).
- Brown under the broiler.
- Garnish each portion with 1 cheese crouton.
- (This method is less expensive because it uses much less cheese.)

17. French Onion Soup Modified From Sandra Lee Recipe

Serving: 10 | Prep: | Cook: 60mins | Ready in:

Ingredients

- 5 med - large white onions, sliced
- 5 med - large yellow onions, sliced
- 3 T chopped garlic
- 4 T worcestershire sauce
- 1 package beefy onion mushroom soup mix
- 1 carton beef broth
- 1/2 carton chicken broth
- 1/2 - 1 c water
- 1/2 stick margarine
- seasoned salt
- garlic pepper
- 3 T dried parsley
- 1 bay leaf
- 2 T cornstarch and 1/4 c water if needed to thicken
- Nice, large, seasoned croutons (homemade ffrom leftover french or itialian bread are best)
- gruyere cheese

Direction

- Mix all ingredients except cheese, croutons, cornstarch and 1/4 c water in large stovetop pot
- Bring to Boil
- Cover, and allow to gently boil 20-30 minutes, stirring occasionally
- Remove lid and simmer, allowing to reduce and thicken
- (Add beef stock, or seasoning as needed, as cooking time progresses)
- Allow to simmer until 15 minutes till serving time
- If needed at this time, mix cornstarch in 1/4 c water and pour into boiling soup
- Stir constantly until thickened slightly
- Ladle soup into individual, oven proof bowls
- Place bowls on baking sheet
- Add Croutons to each bowl
- Cover each with a slice or handful of shredded Gruyere Cheese
- Broil until cheese is melted

18. French Onion Soup Recipe

Serving: 4 | Prep: | Cook: 45mins | Ready in:

Ingredients

- 1 each yellow, white and red onion, sliced
- 2 Tbsp. garlic, crushed
- 2 Tbsp. olive oil
- 1/2 cup dry white wine
- 3 Tbsp. sherry
- 2 Tbsp. all-purpose flour
- 1-1/2 cups chicken broth
- 1-1/2 cups beef broth
- 1 spring thyme
- salt and pepper to taste
- toasted baguettes slices
- 1-1/2 cup swiss cheese, divided
- 1/2 cup Parmesan, shredded, divided

Direction

- Sweat onions and garlic in oil in large pot over medium heat, covered for 10 minutes. Uncover, increase heat to medium high and cook until onion is caramelized, stirring for 20 minutes
- Deglaze with wine and sherry.
- Increase heat to high and simmer to evaporate liquids, stirring often. Stir in flour and cook 1 minute longer.
- Add broths and rhyme, simmer 10 minutes, season with salt and pepper and remove the thyme sprig.
- Preheat the broiler to high.
- Divide the soup among 4 oven safe bowls, top each with baguette slices and some cheeses.
- Place bowls on a baking sheet lined with non-stick foil and broil until golden, 3 to 4 minutes.

19. French Roasted Onion Soup With Thyme Recipe

Serving: 6 | Prep: | Cook: 25mins | Ready in:

Ingredients

- 4 or 5 large Spanish onions (yellow onions) cut lengthwise into thin strips (about 8 cups)
- 8 garlic cloves, minced or pressed
- 1-2 t salt
- 2 T olive oil
- 4 bay leaves
- 1 T dried thyme (or more to taste)
- about 2/3 cup dry white wine
- 8 cups vegetable stock (of course homemade is best, but any will do!)
- 2 T tamari or soy sauce
- salt and ground black pepper to taste
- Optional topping: grated gruyere or swiss cheese and herbed croûtons

Direction

- Preheat oven to 375
- In two shallow baking pans, large enough to spread the onions in one layer, combine onions, garlic, salt, oil, bay leaves, and thyme
- Roast for about 45 minutes, stirring every 15 minutes until the onions have softened and lightly browned.
- Remove onions from oven, add the wine to the pans, and stir with a spoon (wooden works great) to deglaze
- Transfer onion mixture to soup pot
- Add stock and soy sauce
- Cover pot, bring to a boil
- Lower heat and gently simmer for about 25 minutes
- Discard bay leaves and add salt and pepper to taste
- Optionally top each bowl with grated gruyere or Swiss cheese and herbed croutons
- Enjoy!

20. Golden French Onion Soup Recipe

Serving: 4 | Prep: | Cook: 120mins | Ready in:

Ingredients

- 1 qt (approx.)reduced veggie stock/ Strained and simmering on back burner
- 2or 3 yellow onions/ peeled and sliced thin
- 2cloves garlic/ smashed but whole
- bayleaf
- fresh thyme/ a sprig or two left whole
- sprig of rosemary
- any other whole fresh herbs you might have
- 4 thick slices of swiss (or havarti) cheese
- 4 garlic herb croutons (see recipe)
- butter for sauteing
- salt pepper to taste
- 1T(approx) veggie boullion (optional)
- 4 french soup crocks with a dab of butter in the bottom of each

Direction

- Croutons...take four slices of stale French bread/ coat both sides with melted garlic butter and sprinkle with whatever herbs you use in soup.
- Bake in 350 oven till crisp and a bit browned. Flip to get both sides crisp. After you take them out of the oven, sprinkle tops with a good grated cheese like asiago and set aside.
- In the bottom of a two qt. pot
- sauté garlic and sliced onions in butter with the bay leaf over medium low heat till soft and liquid is caramelized add small amounts of stock if things start looking dry...watch closely so the onions don't scorch.
- When you're thinking it needs about another 5 minutes or so, pull out the whole garlic pieces (and eat them)
- Throw in your fresh herbs and bullion if you're using it
- Stir these around with the onions till you can smell the herbs releasing their aromas and the caramelizing is looking good
- Deglaze the pot with the veggie stock.
- Reduce the heat and hold it just below a simmer for about 20 minutes or so to let things marry. Test for salt pepper and adjust to your liking
- Add some of the onion to each crock. Removing any whole herbs as they come up.
- Fill each crock with broth to about 1/2 inch from top. Add crouton and top with cheese. Cheese shouldn't sink into broth. Add more broth if needed to prevent this.
- I hope I didn't forget anything.
- Put in hot 425F oven (or under broiler) long enough to melt the cheese.

21. Guinness French Onion Soup Recipe

Serving: 812 | Prep: | Cook: 3mins | Ready in:

Ingredients

- 1 gallon of cold water
- 8 large Spanish onions
- 1 tablespoon olive oil
- 1-1/2 ounces beef base
- 1-1/2 ounces chicken consomme
- 1 teaspoon basil, chopped
- 1/2 ounce garlic, chopped
- 20 ounces Guinness draught beer (plus some for imbibing!)
- salt and pepper
- provolone cheese slices, 2 per serving bowl
- Homemade croutons:
- stale bread, preferably round, cut into 1-1/2 inch cubes
- butter
- parmesan cheese, grated
- salt
- pepper
- oregano

Direction

- Slice onions lengthwise to form strips.
- Mix with 1 tablespoon olive oil and garlic.
- In a large saucepan, cook onion mixture on low heat until onions are soft.

- In a large stock pot, bring 1 gallon of water to a boil.
- At a boil, and beef base and chicken consommé.
- Mix in basil and stir well.
- Add cooked onions with garlic and oil, directly into water mixture.
- Return to a boil.
- When boiling begins, add Guinness.
- Return to a boil and then let cool.
- Add salt and pepper to taste.
- Croutons:
- Melt butter in microwave or saucepan.
- In a bowl, add bread cubes and pour butter over top. Season with salt, pepper, oregano and a sprinkle of parmesan cheese.
- Toast croutons in a 425° until lightly brown and crisp.
- To serve soup, put into a heat-safe soup bowl. Top with croutons and 2 slices provolone cheese.
- Put bowl(s) on a cookie sheet and bake in a 425° oven for 2-4 minutes until soup heats and cheese browns.

22. Hearty French Onion Soup Recipe

Serving: 4 | Prep: | Cook: 33mins | Ready in:

Ingredients

- 3 large onions, peeled, sliced and separated into rings.
- 2 tablespoons of butter
- 2 cans of condensed beef broth (10.5 oz)
- 1 tablespoon A1 steak sauce
- 1 cup seasoned croutons
- 1 cup shredded mozzarella cheese or shredded swiss cheese

Direction

- Melt butter in large saucepan on medium heat.
- Add onions and cook 10 min or until golden brown, stirring frequently.
- Add broth, 2 soup cans of water and steak sauce.
- Bring to a boil. Reduce heat to medium low and simmer 5 minutes.
- Preheat broiler. Ladle soup evenly into 4 large oven proof bowls.
- Top with croutons and cheese.
- Broil 2 or 3 minutes or until cheese is melted.

23. Julia Child French Onion Soup Recipe

Serving: 6 | Prep: | Cook: 90mins | Ready in:

Ingredients

- 2 tablespoons butter
- 1/4 cup olive oil
- 3 lbs onions, halved and sliced thin
- 2 cloves garlic, minced very fine
- 1 teaspoon granulated sugar
- 2 cups dry white wine
- 6 cups beef stock or chicken stock (the beef will make a darker, more robust soup)
- salt and freshly ground black pepper
- 6 ovenproof soup bowls
- 12 toasted slices of French baguettes, 1/2 inch thick
- 2 cups swiss cheese, grated
- 3 teaspoons parmesan cheese, grated

Direction

- In a large saucepan over medium heat melt the butter and oil together.
- Add the onions, garlic, and sugar. Sauté until slightly colored, stirring occasionally (don't stir too much - you want them to brown), for 7 minutes.
- Add the white wine, raise temperature to medium high, and bring to a boil.
- Lower temperature back down to medium and cook for 5 minutes.

- Add the stock, raise temperature to medium high and bring to a simmer.
- Lower temperature to low and simmer *uncovered* for 1 1/2 hours (90 minutes).
- At this point you can freeze the soup for reheating later (after thawing).
- To serve at this point, continue with steps: first, preheat your broiler.
- Ladle the soup into the ovenproof soup bowls (6 of them).
- Place two slices of toasted baguette onto the top of each soup bowl.
- Sprinkle each serving with 1/3 cup of Swiss cheese, then 1/2 teaspoon of Parmesan cheese.
- Place soup bowls onto a baking sheet and place in oven under preheated broiler.
- Broil until the cheese melts (watch them carefully - depending on your broiler and how far the rack is from the heat, it can take anywhere to 45 to 90 seconds or so).
- Serve immediately.

24. Julia Childs French Onion Soup Grantineed With Cheese Recipe

Serving: 6 | Prep: | Cook: 75mins | Ready in:

Ingredients

- 1 1/2 lbs (about 5 cups or a little more) thinly sliced yellow onions
- 3 T. butter... See More
- 1 T. vegetable oil
- A heavy-bottomed, 4-quart covered saucepan
- 1 t. salt
- 1/4 t. sugar (helps the onions to brown)
- 3 T. flour
- 2 quarts boiling brown stock, purchased beef stock, or 1 quart of water and 1 quart of stock
- 1/2 c. dry white wine or dry white vermouth
- salt and pepper to taste
- 2 oz. (about 3/4 c.) shredded swiss cheese
- 1 T. grated raw onion
- 8 to 10 rounds of hard toasted French bread (toast bread rounds in oven at 225 for 25 min.)
- For bread Rounds:
- 1 1/2 c. grated Swiss, or Swiss and parmesan cheese
- 1 T. olive oil or melted butter

Direction

- Cook the onions slowly with the butter and oil in the covered saucepan for 15 minutes.
- Uncover, raise heat to moderate, and stir in the salt and sugar. Cook for 30 to 40 minutes stirring frequently, until the onions have turned an even, deep, golden brown.
- Sprinkle in the flour and stir for 3 minutes.
- Off heat, blend in the boiling liquid. Add the wine, and season to taste. Simmer partially covered for 30 to 40 minutes or more, skimming occasionally. Correct seasoning.
- Preheat the oven to 325 degrees.
- Bring the soup to the boil and pour into a tureen or soup pots. Stir in the 3/4 c. shredded Swiss cheese and grated onion. Float the rounds of toast on top of the soup, and spread the grated cheese over it. Sprinkle with the oil or butter.
- Bake for 20 minutes in the oven, then set for a minute or two under a preheated broiler to brown the top lightly. Serve immediately.

25. Mediterranean Style French Onion Soup Recipe

Serving: 0 | Prep: | Cook: 2hours | Ready in:

Ingredients

- 6 large Red/White/ Spanish Onions (or a combination of them) - peeled and thinly sliced - BEST - use all three
- Extra Virgin Olive Oil - to taste re cooking the onions
- 1/4 tsp Sugar – to taste
- 2 cloves Garlic - minced

- 1.8ltrs/4 pints/beef stock
- 125ml/4fl oz dry White Wine
- 1 Bay Leaf
- ½tsp dried Thyme
- Salt and freshly ground black pepper
- 8 slices Baguette - sliced and toasted
- 12oz/360g Swiss Gruyere cheese plus 2oz/60g Parmesan cheese - grated and mixed together

Direction

- In a large saucepan, add the oil, heat on a very low heat and sauté the onions, stirring often, for some 2 hours or so or until well, well browned (caramelised) but not burned;
- Add the sugar about 15 minutes or so into the process to help with the browning (caramelization);
- When satisfied re caramelization, add the garlic and sauté for about 1 minute then add the stock, vermouth (or wine), bay leaf, and thyme;
- Bring to boil, partially cover and simmer about 30 minutes until the flavours are well blended;
- Season to taste with salt and pepper;
- Discard the bay leaf;
- To serve, ladle the soup into individual oven-proof soup bowls or a large casserole dish; Cover with the toast and sprinkle on the cheese to cover the toast to taste;
- Either place straight under a very hot grill for a few minutes or place into a broiler at 180c/350f/gas 4 for about 10 minutes until the cheese bubbles and is slightly browned and golden;
- Serve immediately.

26. Mellissa D'arabian's French Onion Soup Recipe

Serving: 4 | Prep: | Cook: 2hours | Ready in:

Ingredients

- 2 tablespoons butter
- 4 yellow onions (about 1 3/4 pounds), thinly sliced with the grain to hold their shape
- kosher salt and freshly ground black pepper
- 1 teaspoon flour
- 1/2 cup dry red wine
- 1 tablespoon chopped fresh thyme
- 1 bay leaf
- 1 teaspoon lemon juice
- 2 cups beef stock
- 2 cups chicken stock
- 1/2 cup grated Swiss
- 1 tablespoon grated Parmesan
- 4 (1-inch thick) baguette slices, cut on the bias

Direction

- In a heavy bottomed Dutch oven or large saucepan, melt the butter over medium-low heat. Add the onions, sprinkle with salt, cover, and cook until deeply caramelized, 1 to 1 1/2 hours. Turn the heat up to medium and sprinkle the onions with the flour. Stir and allow to cook for 1 or 2 minutes. Deglaze the pan with the red wine. Add the thyme, bay leaf, lemon juice, and stock and simmer for 10 minutes. Taste and add salt and pepper, as needed. Ladle the soup into 4 ovenproof crocks.
- Heat the broiler to high. Mix the cheeses together in a small bowl. Top each crock with a baguette slice and evenly distribute the cheese on top of each. Place the crocks under the broiler just until the cheese is bubbly and browning, about 1 minute. Serve hot

27. Onion Soup With Champagne Recipe

Serving: 2 | Prep: | Cook: 20mins | Ready in:

Ingredients

- 2 large onions
- 1 quart dry champagne
- 1 garlic clove

- chopped parsley
- 20 blanched almonds
- Sliced French bread
- Parmesean cheese

Direction

- Slice the onions very thin and fry them lightly in butter.
- Pour on the onions the champagne.
- Add the parsley, almonds and garlic - put the garlic on a toothpick to make it easy to remove later.
- Boil for 20 minutes and remove the garlic.
- Place a slice of French bread in the bottom of each bowl, and ladle the soup over.
- Sprinkle with Parmesan cheese.

28. Paula Deens French Onion Soup Recipe

Serving: 7 | Prep: | Cook: 45mins | Ready in:

Ingredients

- 8 onions, sliced
- 2 cloves garlic, minced
- 1/3 cup olive oil
- 2 tablespoons all-purpose flour
- 8 cups beef stock
- 1/4 cup dry white wine
- 1/2 teaspoon dried thyme
- 1 bay leaf
- salt and pepper
- 1 loaf French bread
- 2 cups grated gruyere

Direction

- Sauté onions and garlic in oil over low heat until tender and golden yellow.
- Sprinkle flour over onions, cook a few minutes more, browning the flour well.
- Add stock and wine and bring to a boil, add thyme and bay leaf. Reduce heat, cover, and simmer gently for 20 minutes or so.
- Add salt and pepper, to taste.
- Meanwhile, slice French bread into 3/4-inch slices and butter both sides.
- Toast slices on griddle until golden brown.
- Ladle soup into an ovenproof bowl, add toasted bread and cover with cheese.
- Place ovenproof bowl on a baking sheet lined with tin foil.
- Bake at 350 degrees F or 5 minutes under a hot broiler

29. Rather French Onion Soup Recipe

Serving: 6 | Prep: | Cook: 3hours | Ready in:

Ingredients

- 1/4 cup butter
- 1 tbsp rendered bacon fat (or canola oil)
- 8 large onions, thinly sliced into "half-moons" (approx 3 lbs)
- 1/2 tsp kosher salt
- 1/2 tsp brown sugar
- 1 tbsp flour (you can use rice flour for GF)
- 8 cups low-sodium beef stock, hot
- 1 sprig fresh thyme (or 1 tsp dried)
- 1/4 cup cognac
- 1 cup dry white wine (we used a French Sauvignon Blanc)
- 6 thick slices of French bread, cut to the size of the serving bowls and toasted (use GF French bread if needed)
- 1 1/2 cups coarsely grated Gruyère (for a true French soup, use Comté)

Direction

- Heat a heavy saucepan over medium-low heat with the butter and bacon fat.
- Stir in the onions and cover.

- Cook slowly, stirring once or twice, until onions are tender and translucent, about 12 minutes.
- Stir in the salt and sugar, increase the heat to medium, and let the onions cook, stirring just enough to prevent burning, until brown (25 to 30 minutes).
- Sprinkle the flour and cook slowly, stirring constantly, for another 3 to 4 minutes.
- Remove from heat and whisk in 2 cups of hot stock.
- Return to the heat and bring to a simmer, adding the rest of the stock, thyme, Cognac, and wine.
- Cover and simmer over low heat for 1 1/2 hours.
- Remove thyme sprig and simmer a further 15 minutes, adding a little water if the liquid reduces too much. Taste for seasoning.
- Divide the soup between 6 ovenproof bowls.
- Arrange toast on top of soup and sprinkle 1/4 cup of grated cheese on top of each croute.
- Place bowls on a baking sheet and place under a preheated broiler until cheese melts and forms a crust over the tops of the bowls.
- Serve immediately.

30. Simple French Onion Soup Recipe

Serving: 8 | Prep: | Cook: 2hours | Ready in:

Ingredients

- 6 large yellow or red onions, thinly sliced (I sometimes use a combo of both)
- 3 tbls. olive oil
- 1/2 cup dry white wine or dry sherry
- 1/2 tsp. sugar
- 1/4-1/2 tsp. dried thyme
- 1 bay leaf
- 8 cups beef broth
- 2 cloves garlic, minced
- salt and pepper to taste
- 1 1/2 cups gruyere cheese, grated
- 8 slices French bread, cubed and toasted

Direction

- Over medium heat, add oil to heat.
- Add onions, salt and pepper.
- Cook, stirring occasionally
- After 10 minutes add sugar and stir to combine
- Cook another 15-20 minutes until onions are caramelized
- Add garlic and cook for a minute
- Add wine or sherry, thyme and bay leaf
- Stir to combine
- Add beef broth, stir to combine
- Cover pan partially and simmer for half an hour
- Season with salt and pepper
- Remove bay leaf
- Ladle soup into ovenproof soup bowls
- Top each one with toasted croutons
- Sprinkle gruyere top of croutons
- Bake in oven at 400 until cheese is bubbling and melted

31. Super Easy French Onion Soup Recipe

Serving: 4 | Prep: | Cook: 20mins | Ready in:

Ingredients

- 2 cans of Campbell's onion soup
- 2 cans of water
- 1 pkg. of Lipton's French onion soup
- 1 Tablespoon of worchestershire sauce
- 1/4 cup parmasean cheese
- croutons
- mozza cheese (however much you like, i use 1/2 a block)

Direction

- In a saucepan stir all ingredients together except for croutons and mozza cheese.
- Bring to a boil stirring constantly for about 3 minutes.
- Pour into individual oven safe bowls.
- Sprinkle with croutons and place mozza cheese on top.
- Bake in 350 degree oven till cheese melts then broil until cheese is browned.

32. Tomato French Onion Soup Recipe

Serving: 4 | Prep: | Cook: 15mins | Ready in:

Ingredients

- 4 large sweet onions, peeled and sliced
- 2 tablespoons butter
- 1 (14 1/2 ounce) can diced tomatoes, undrained
- 2 cups water
- 1 can beef consomme
- 1/4 cup dry red wine
- 4 slices French or Italian bread, toasted
- mozzarella cheese, shredded

Direction

- In large saucepan, sauté onions in butter until softened.
- Add tomatoes with liquid, water, consommé and wine.
- Bring to a boil, skimming off any "foam" that collects.
- Reduce heat and simmer 10 minutes.
- Place bread in the bottom of 4 oven-proof bowls.
- Ladle soup over bread.
- Cover with cheese.
- Place soup bowls under broiler until cheese is melted and just slightly browned around the edges.

33. Tyler Florences French Onion Soup Recipe

Serving: 8 | Prep: | Cook: 40mins | Ready in:

Ingredients

- /2 cup unsalted butter
- 4 onions, sliced
- 2 garlic cloves, chopped
- 2 bay leaves
- 2 fresh thyme sprigs
- kosher salt and freshly ground black pepper
- 1 cup red wine, about 1/2 bottle
- 3 heaping tablespoons all-purpose flour
- 2 quarts beef broth
- 1 baguette, sliced
- 1/2 pound grated gruyere

Direction

- Melt the stick of butter in a large pot over medium heat. Add the onions, garlic, bay leaves, thyme, and salt and pepper and cook until the onions are very soft and caramelized, about 25 minutes. Add the wine, bring to a boil, reduce the heat and simmer until the wine has evaporated and the onions are dry, about 5 minutes. Discard the bay leaves and thyme sprigs. Dust the onions with the flour and give them a stir. Turn the heat down to medium low so the flour doesn't burn, and cook for 10 minutes to cook out the raw flour taste. Now add the beef broth, bring the soup back to a simmer, and cook for 10 minutes. Season, to taste, with salt and pepper.
- When you're ready to eat, preheat the broiler. Arrange the baguette slices on a baking sheet in a single layer. Sprinkle the slices with the Gruyere and broil until bubbly and golden brown, 3 to 5 minutes.
- Ladle the soup in bowls and float several of the Gruyere croutons on top.

34. Vegetarian French Onion Recipe

Serving: 6 | Prep: | Cook: 4mins | Ready in:

Ingredients

- 3 red onions
- 3 white onions
- 1.5 litres veggie stock
- 750 ml of cheap burgandy
- 4 buds fresh garlic
- 1/2 a stick of butter
- salt, pepper to taste
- French bread
- shredded swizz and mozza

Direction

- Thinly slice all of the onions, a food processor works great
- Dice garlic
- Sauté garlic and onions in fry pan on low heat to caramelize the onions
- Combine all items into a crock pot or stock pot
- Salt and pepper to taste
- Heat to boil then reduce and simmer
- Toast some French bread under the broiler
- Put the soup in bowls
- Top with the toasted bread and cheese and broil again to melt cheese

35. Vegetarian French Onion Soup Recipe

Serving: 6 | Prep: | Cook: 60mins | Ready in:

Ingredients

- 2 tbsp butter
- 1 tbsp vegetable oil
- 5 large onions, thinly sliced
- 1 tsp sugar
- 1 tsp salt, plus a bit more to finish
- 2 tbsp all-purpose flour
- 6 cups vegetable broth (homemade or canned, I may include a recipe at a later time)
- 1/3 cup dry sherry
- 1 1/2 tsp fresh thyme, chopped, or 1/2 tsp dried
- black pepper to taste
- 6 1/2 inch slices of French bread
- 6 slices of a white, melting cheese (I used swiss) or 2 1/2 cups grated cheese (gruyere or Jarlsberg are pretty tradtional)

Direction

- In a pot over medium heat, melt the butter and the oil.
- Add the onions, sugar, and salt and cook for 1 minute while stirring.
- Reduce heat to medium-low and cook, stirring occasionally, until the onions have caramelized, which should take anywhere from 20 - 40 minutes
- Add the flour and cook while stirring for 1 minute
- Add the broth, sherry, and thyme and bring to a boil.
- Reduce heat and simmer for 15 minutes.
- Season to taste with the salt and pepper.
- Preheat the broiler and broil the slices of bread until lightly toasted. Add butter to the bread if you'd like.
- Put the soup in 6 ovenproof bowls and set them on a baking sheet.
- Cover with the bread slices, which you may need to cut to fit.
- Put the cheese on top of the bread slices.
- Put the baking sheet under the broiler until the cheese is melted and bubbly.

36. French Onion Soup Recipe

Serving: 4 | Prep: | Cook: 45mins | Ready in:

Ingredients

- 1 large yellow onion

- 1 red onion
- 1 box beef broth
- 1 lemon
- salt
- pepper
- yellow mustard seed
- celery seed
- crusty good French bread
- good swiss cheese

Direction

- I put my onions in the freezer so I don't cry like a baby
- Cut onion in half then into thin stripes
- Cook over medium heat and a huge tap of butter for about 10 min with all salt pepper and mustard and celery
- then put heat up to medium high to high and cook stirring until they look dark caramel colour and are completely cooked then add your box broth usually 32 oz., then fill half way up with water and pour that all in, let this come to a boil for 30 min so you are left with a thick clear broth and tender but not mushy onion cause we caramelized them
- Cut your crusty bread into angled slices so there is more surface area for cheese
- toast them under broiler until both sides are brown and delish, then put lots and lots and lots if you're like me, then put back only for a min, so it get all gooey but not brown so it goes through that hot broth and makes it all cheesy, oh so good!! But make sure everyone eats this because you get bad breath with the onions and Swiss, lol

Chapter 2: Awesome Onion Soup Recipes

***

37. Angel Hair And Three Onion Soup Recipe

Serving: 4 | Prep: | Cook: 90mins | Ready in:

Ingredients

- 4 Tbsp olive oil
- 1/2 lb baby (pearl) onions, fresh (or ½ frozen bag, thawed)
- 1 medium red onion, sliced thin
- 1 medium vidalia onion (or other sweet onion), sliced thin
- 6 cups (48 fl oz) chicken stock
- salt (to taste)
- 1/4 tsp red pepper flakes
- 1/2 lb angel hair pasta, broken in 2-inch pieces
- 1/4 cup chopped flat leaf parsley
- 4 tsp grated romano cheese

Direction

- PLACE oil and all onions in a large sauce pan over low heat and sauté, stirring occasionally, about 20 minutes, until onions are golden.
- Add stock and salt to taste.
- Sprinkle with red pepper flakes and simmer for about 1 hour.
- ADD pasta and parsley and cook until pasta is just al dente.
- LADLE into soup bowls.
- Sprinkle with grated Romano cheese

38. Asparagus Soup Puree With Green Onion Recipe

Serving: 4 | Prep: | Cook: 15mins | Ready in:

Ingredients

- 2 scallions cut into 1 inch pieces
- 1/2 medium onion - chopped
- 1/4 teaspoon black pepper

- 3/4 teaspoon salt
- 1 tablespoons unsalted butter
- 1 tablespoon olive oil
- 2 1/2 lb asparagus, trimmed and cut into 1 1/2-inch pieces
- 3 1/2 chicken broth
- 1 1/2 cups water

Direction

- Heat oil and melt butter together in a 4-6 quart pot.
- Cook onion over moderately low heat, stirring, until onion is softened, about 3 minutes.
- Add scallion and 1/2 the salt and sauté about one more minute.
- Add asparagus, broth, and simmer, covered, until asparagus is just tender, 10 to 12 minutes.
- Purée soup in batches in a blender/food processor until smooth- *I use a slotted spoon to remove all the solids and puree them separately-this way I can puree it all in one shot.
- Return puree to pot with liquid and add water.
- Stir in remaining salt and pepper to taste (pepper is optional) and heat through.
- *serve with shaved parmesan cheese curls or parmesan toasts if desired

39. Aztec Onion And Lime Soup With Blue Corn Dumplings Recipe

Serving: 8 | Prep: | Cook: 45mins | Ready in:

Ingredients

- 3 tablespoons corn oil
- 4 medium yellow onions thinly sliced
- 5 garlic cloves finely chopped
- 3 jalapenos seeded chopped fine
- 1 large tomato peeled seeded and chopped
- 5 cups chicken stock
- 1/4 cup lime juice
- 1 tablespoon finely grated lime zest
- 1 teaspoon salt
- 1 teaspoon freshly ground black pepper
- Dumplings:
- 1 cup blue corn flour
- 2 teaspoons baking powder
- 1 teaspoon salt
- 2 tablespoons vegetable shortening
- 1 egg
- 1/2 cup milk
- 2 tablespoons finely chopped cilantro

Direction

- Over low heat warm corn oil in a large heavy pot.
- Add onions and stir to coat them with oil.
- Cover and cook slowly for 20 minutes.
- Uncover pot and raise heat to medium.
- Stir in the garlic and jalapenos then sauté for 2 minutes.
- Add tomato and continue to cook stirring for 1 more minute.
- Add stock, lime juice, zest, salt and pepper.
- Bring to a boil then lower the heat and simmer uncovered for 30 minutes.
- Meanwhile prepare the dumplings by sifting the corn flour, baking powder and salt into a medium sized bowl.
- Using your fingers, two knives or a pastry cutter cut in the vegetable shortening until mixture resembles fine crumbs.
- In a small bowl beat together the egg and milk then add the cilantro.
- Gradually stir the egg mixture into the corn flour mixture adding only enough of the egg to moisten the flour thoroughly.
- When the soup has cooked for 30 minutes drop the dough into the simmering broth a tablespoon at a time to make a dozen dumplings.
- Cover the pot with a tight-fitting lid, and steam the dumplings for 15 minutes.
- Keep the soup at a low bubble and do not lift the lid while the dumplings are cooking.
- Serve hot.

40. Baked Onion Soup Recipe

Serving: 8 | Prep: | Cook: 30mins | Ready in:

Ingredients

- 2 tablespoons canola oil
- 8 medium onions quartered and thinly sliced
- 2 cloves garlic minced
- 5 cups water
- 1/4 cup dry red wine
- 1 teaspoon dry mustard
- 4 tablespoons miso dissolved in 1/3 cup water
- French bread
- 1-1/2 cups grated mozzarella cheese

Direction

- Heat oil in a soup pot then add onions and sauté over medium heat until golden.
- Add garlic and continue to sauté slowly until onions are lightly and evenly browned.
- Add water, wine and mustard then bring to a simmer and simmer gently covered for 15 minutes.
- Stir in the dissolved miso and remove soup from heat and allow soup to stand 15 minutes.
- Preheat oven to 350 then slice bread into 1" thick slices then bake on cookie sheet 15 minutes.
- Place a slice of bread in each ovenproof bowl and ladle serving of soup over it.
- Sprinkle 1/4 cup of the grated cheese over each then place bowls on 2 cookie sheets.
- Bake soup 10 minutes then serve immediately.

41. Banana And Onion Soup Recipe

Serving: 68 | Prep: | Cook: 1mins | Ready in:

Ingredients

- 6 bananas, peeled, sliced
- 4 onions, peeled, sliced thin
- 2 cups milk, scalded
- 3 cups water, boiling
- 2 tablespoons butter
- seasonings to taste

Direction

- Boil all ingredients together for about 25 minutes.
- Pass through a sieve.
- Put soup back in stew pan, boil for 1 minute, and then serve.

42. Beef Jerky And Onion Soup Recipe

Serving: 4 | Prep: | Cook: 40mins | Ready in:

Ingredients

- 3 tablespoons olive oil
- 4 large white onions chopped
- 2 tablespoons paprika
- 1 winter squash chopped
- 1/2 pound beef jerky chopped
- 1 teaspoon cumin
- 1 teaspoon oregano
- 6 cups beef broth
- 1/2 teaspoon salt
- 1 teaspoon freshly ground black pepper
- 8 medium eggs
- 2 tablespoons parsley chopped
- 1 lemon juiced
- 1 large juiced

Direction

- Sauté onion, squash and paprika in oil for 10 minutes.
- Add jerky, cumin, oregano and broth then simmer 25 minutes.
- Season with salt and pepper.
- Poach eggs in water for 5 minutes.

- Stir lemon juice and orange juice into soup then simmer 1 minute.
- Place an egg in a soup bowl then top with soup and sprinkle with parsley and serve.

43. Beef And Onion Stew Stifado Recipe

Serving: 4 | Prep: | Cook: 120mins | Ready in:

Ingredients

- 1 medium onion, chopped
- 2 cloves garlic, minced
- 3 tablespoons olive oil
- 1 (2 pound) boneless beef chuck, tip or round, cut into 1-inch cubes
- 1/2 cup dry red wine
- 2 tablespoons red wine vinegar
- 1/2 teaspoon salt
- 1/4 teaspoon coarsely-ground pepper
- 1 bay leaf
- 1 stick cinnamon
- 1 (8 ounce) can tomato sauce
- 1 1/2 pound pearl onions, peeled
- Crumbled feta cheese

Direction

- Cook and stir chopped onion and garlic in oil in Dutch oven over medium heat until onion is tender; remove with slotted spoon.
- Cook beef in remaining oil, stirring frequently, until all liquid is evaporated and beef is brown on all sides, about 25 minutes; drain fat.
- Return onion and garlic to Dutch oven. Stir in remaining ingredients except onions and cheese. Heat to boiling; reduce heat. Cover and simmer 1 hour and 15 minutes.
- Add white onions. Cover and simmer until beef and white onions are tender, about 30 minutes. Remove bay leaf and cinnamon. Garnish with cheese.

44. Beer, Onion And Carrot Soup Recipe

Serving: 0 | Prep: | Cook: 45mins | Ready in:

Ingredients

- 1/2 cup shredded sharp cheddar cheese
- 4 tbs butter
- 2 tbs flour
- French bread, sliced into small pieces
- 1 12oz bottle of good brown ale
- 3 cups beef stock
- 1 large carrot, shredded
- 2 large onions, thinly sliced
- 2 garlic cloves, minced
- 1 tbs honey
- 1/4 cup sherry
- worcestershire sauce, to taste (I use a couple splashes)
- salt and black pepper, to taste
- hot sauce of your choice, to taste
- 1/4 cup heavy cream, if needed/desired.

Direction

- Toast the bread pieces in the oven at 375 degrees until just barely browned. Remove, sprinkle the cheese on the slices, return to the oven and cook until the cheese just melts. Set the bread aside.
- Melt the butter in a large sauce pan on medium heat. Add the onions and cook, stirring occasionally to keep them from burning, for about 10 minutes. The onions should achieve a golden brown colour and very soft texture.
- Add the garlic and carrots and cook for five more minutes.
- Add the flour and cook for another minute to create a sort of "paste" with the vegetables.
- Add the beer, stock, honey, sherry, Worcestershire sauce, seasonings and hot sauce. Bring to a simmer. Let the soup simmer

for another 10 minutes, or until it starts to thicken slightly.
- If you would like it a bit thicker and creamier, lower the heat and add in the 1/4 of cream. Not necessary, it's equally delicious without it. Adjust your seasonings if needed.
- Serve with the "croutons" on the side. Add them in when it's time to eat for a hint of cheese and texture.

45. Bennigans Onion Soup Copycat Recipe

Serving: 8 | Prep: | Cook: 10mins | Ready in:

Ingredients

- 1/2 Pound Firm white onions -- sliced
- 1/4 Cup butter
- 2 Tablespoons corn oil
- 3 Tablespoons flour
- 1 Quart chicken broth
- 1 Quart beef broth
- 8 French bread Slices
- swiss cheese -- shredded
- Parmesan -- grated

Direction

- Sauté onions in butter and oil until onions are transparent, but not well browned.
- When tender, turn heat to lowest point and sprinkle with flour, stirring vigorously.
- Pour into Dutch oven and stir in broths. Heat thoroughly and divide among 8 oven-proof bowls.
- Float a slice of bread atop each serving. Mix equal parts of cheese to smooth paste and spread over bread.
- Place all bowls on oven rack 4" from broiler heat and broil until cheese melts.
- Serve at once.

46. Booming Onion Rhubarb Soup Recipe

Serving: 4 | Prep: | Cook: 15mins | Ready in:

Ingredients

- 1 medium orange
- 2 pounds rhubarb
- 1 cup sugar
- 4 cups water
- 3 tablespoons sour cream

Direction

- Zest orange and mince zest then juice the orange.
- Remove string from rhubarb then chop rhubarb.
- Combine rhubarb, sugar, water, orange juice and half the zest in saucepan and bring to a boil.
- Turn heat to medium and cook 15 minutes.
- Chill and serve.

47. Buttermilk Bisque With Cucumbers And Onions Recipe

Serving: 4 | Prep: | Cook: | Ready in:

Ingredients

- 3 cups chopped cucumber
- 1/2 cup chopped vidalia onions
- 2 tablespoons chopped fresh dill, plus more for garnish
- 1 quart buttermilk
- 1 cup plain yogurt
- 2 teaspoons sugar
- salt and pepper to taste

Direction

- Place ingredients in a food processor fitted with a metal blade or blender and puree until almost smooth.
- Chill at least one hour before serving.
- Garnish with additional dill.

48. Cams Onion Soup Recipe

Serving: 6 | Prep: | Cook: 90mins | Ready in:

Ingredients

- - 1/4 cup of butter (unsalted)
- - 6 medium onions (approx 2 - 2 1/2 lbs) thinly sliced
- - 1 clove of garlic, finely diced
- - 1 tsp of sugar
- - 6 - 8 tsp of flour
- - 8 cups of beef broth (may add more water depending on saltiness of broth)
- - 1 tsp of Dijon mustard or 1 tsp dried mustard
- - 1/4 tsp of nutmeg
- - 3 tsp of worcestershire sauce
- - 1/2 to 1/4 cup of white wine or few drops of lemon juice to taste
- - 2 cups of croûtons (easy to make; use your favorite bread toasted then diced into crouton squares)
- - Sliced swiss cheese (as desired)
- - parmesan cheese (as desired)

Direction

- - In large kettle, melt butter, add onions, garlic and sprinkle w/ sugar. Sauté over medium heat stirring occasionally for first 30 minutes. Reduce heat and cook till lightly browned (approx. 20 minutes).
- - Sprinkle flour over cooked onions
- - Add broth, Dijon mustard, Nutmeg and Worcestershire sauce
- - Simmer over medium/low heat for 15 minutes
- - Add White Wine (or lemon juice)
- - Ladle into oven-proof crock style bowls till approx. 3/4 full
- - Add croutons
- - Lay out slice of Swiss cheese across croutons
- - Sprinkle on desired amount of Parmesan Cheese on top
- - Place under HI broiler until cheese bubbly and browned ... DO NOT LEAVE UNATTENDED!

49. Canadian Onion Soup Recipe

Serving: 6 | Prep: | Cook: 20mins | Ready in:

Ingredients

- 3 tbsp canola oil
- 4 lb sweet onions, thinly sliced
- 3 cloves garlic, minced
- ½ cup pure maple syrup
- 1 900 ml tetri-pack of fat free beef broth or your own beef broth
- 1 tbsp chopped fresh thyme leaves
- salt & pepper tp taste (or McCormick's NO salt ADDED CITRUS & pepper)
- 6 slices of baguette, toasted
- 2 cups shredded five year old Canadian cheddar cheese

Direction

- Heat oil in a Dutch oven set over medium heat.
- Add onion, and cook, stirring frequently, for 30 minutes, or until well caramelized.
- Add garlic and cook an additional 30 seconds, then stir in the maple syrup.
- Add the broth and half the thyme, and bring to a boil.
- Reduce heat and simmer for 20 minutes.
- Season to taste with salt & pepper as desired.
- Preheat the broiler.
- Divide the soup between 6 oven-proof bowls.
- Top with toast slices and equal amounts of cheese.

- Broil for 2 – 3 minutes, until cheese melts and lightly browns.
- Garnish with remaining thyme and serve.

50. Cantaloupe Honeydew And Sweet Onion Gazpacho With Crispy Prosciutto Recipe

Serving: 6 | Prep: | Cook: 10mins | Ready in:

Ingredients

- ¼ pound thinly sliced proscuitto (or Serrano ham -- see below)
- ¼ cup fresh lemon juice
- ¼ cup fresh lime juice
- 3 slices white bread, crusts removed and cubed
- 2 tablespoons minced jalapeños
- 2 teaspoons minced garlic
- 1 tablespoon finely chopped chives
- 1 tablespoon finely chopped parsley
- 1 tablespoon finely chopped mint
- 1 tablespoon finely chopped cilantro
- ¼ cup extra virgin olive oil
- 1 tablespoon salt
- 1 teaspoon ground black pepper
- 1 cup roughly chopped cantaloupe, plus ¾ cup finely diced cantaloupe
- 1 cup roughly chopped honeydew melon, plus ¾ cup finely diced honeydew melon
- 1 cup roughly chopped sweet onion, such as Vidalia, plus 1 cup finely diced sweet onion
- ½ cup roughly chopped celery, plus ¼ cup finely diced celery
- ½ cup roughly chopped red bell pepper, plus ¼ cup finely diced red bell pepper
- 1 cup roughly chopped, seeded, peeled cucumber, plus ¾ cup finely diced, seeded, peeled cucumber

Direction

- Preheat the oven to 375 degrees F.
- Cover a baking sheet with parchment paper and bake the prosciutto until crisp, about 10 to 12 minutes. Remove from the oven and let cool. [Note: You can also use Serrano ham – drop small slices of the ham into hot oil and deep fry for about a minute just until the ham begins to look like bacon.]
- Combine the roughly chopped ingredients (cantaloupe, honeydew, sweet onion, celery, red bell pepper, and cucumber), lemon juice, lime juice, and bread in blender. Purée on high until smooth.
- Combine the finely chopped ingredients, jalapenos, garlic, chives, parsley, mint, cilantro, and olive oil in a large bowl. Stir well to combine.
- Fold the puréed ingredients into the chopped ingredients.
- Add the salt and pepper and stir well to combine.
- Let rest at least 1 hour, covered and refrigerated, for the flavours to blend.
- Serve chilled, garnished with crumbled crispy prosciutto.

51. Caramelized Onion Portobello Mushroom Soup With Goat Cheese Croutons Recipe

Serving: 6 | Prep: | Cook: 60mins | Ready in:

Ingredients

- 3 tablespoons butter
- 1 1/2 pounds onions, halved, thinly sliced (about 5 cups)
- 4 fresh thyme sprigs
- 1 1/2 pounds portobello mushrooms, stemmed, caps halved and cut crosswise into 1/4-inch-thick strips
- 3 tablespoons cognac or brandy
- 3 garlic cloves, minced
- 8 cups canned vegetable broth
- 1 cup dry white wine

- 18 1-inch-thick slices French-bread baguette, toasted
- 8 ounces soft fresh goat cheese, room temperature

Direction

- Melt 1 tablespoon butter in heavy large pot over high heat.
- Add onions and thyme;
- Sauté until onions begin to soften, about 8 minutes.
- Reduce heat to low; cook until onions are caramelized, stirring occasionally, about 20 minutes.
- Transfer onion mixture to medium bowl.
- Melt remaining 2 tablespoons butter in same pot over medium-high heat.
- Add mushrooms; sauté until soft, about 12 minutes.
- Add Cognac and garlic; stir 20 seconds.
- Stir in onion mixture, then broth and wine.
- Bring to boil.
- Reduce heat to low; simmer until onions are very tender, about 45 minutes.
- Discard thyme sprigs.
- Season soup with salt and pepper.
- Preheat broiler.
- Place baguette slices on large baking sheet.
- Spread goat cheese on baguette slices, dividing equally.
- Broil goat cheese croutons until cheese begins to brown in spots, about 30 seconds.
- Divide soup among 6 bowls.
- Top with croutons and serve. .

52. Caramelized Onion And Parmesan Cheese Soup Recipe

Serving: 6 | Prep: | Cook: 60mins | Ready in:

Ingredients

- 2 tablespoons olive oil
- 2 cups 1-inch sliced onions

- 1/3 cup peeled garlic cloves, (about 12 to 14)
- 2 bay leaves
- 2 1/2 teaspoons salt
- 6 turns fresh black pepper
- 2 quarts chicken stock
- 1 tablespoon minced garlic
- 1 teaspoon fresh chopped basil
- 1 teaspoon fresh chopped thyme
- 2 cups diced day old French bread
- 1/2 cup heavy cream
- 1/2 cup grated parmigiano-reggiano cheese
- 1 tablespoon finely chopped parsley

Direction

- In a soup pot, heat the olive oil.
- When the oil is hot, add the onions, garlic cloves, and bay leaves.
- Season with salt and pepper.
- Sauté the onion mixture until the onions are caramelized, about 7 minutes.
- Stir in the stock, minced garlic, basil, and thyme.
- Bring the liquid up to a boil.
- Reduce to a simmer and simmer for 40 minutes.
- Turn the heat up and whisk in the bread and cream.
- Continue whisking until the bread has dissolved into the soup for about 10 minutes.
- With a hand-held blender, puree the soup until smooth.
- Whisk in the Parmigiano-Reggiano cheese and parsley.
- Season with salt and pepper.

53. Carbonnade A La Flamande Belgian Beef Beer And Onion Stew Recipe

Serving: 6 | Prep: | Cook: 150mins | Ready in:

Ingredients

- 3 1/2 lbs boneless chuck roast or blade steak, trimmed and cut in 1-inch cubes
- salt and pepper
- 4-6 T vegetable oil
- 2 lbs yellow onions (about 3 medium), halved and sliced about 1/4-inch thick (about 8 cups)
- 1 T tomato paste
- 2 medium cloves garlic, minced or pressed through garlic press (about 2 tsp)
- 3 T all-purpose flour
- 3/4 c low-sodium chicken broth
- 3/4 c low-sodium beef broth
- 12 ounce bottle or can of dark or amber ale. (O'Doul's amber non-alcoholic beer works fine)
- 4 sprigs fresh thyme, tied with kitchen twine
- 2 bay leaves
- 1 T cider vinegar

Direction

- Adjust oven rack to lower-middle position; heat oven to 300 degrees. Dry beef thoroughly with paper towels, then season generously with salt and pepper. Heat 2 teaspoons oil in large heavy-bottomed Dutch oven over medium-high heat until beginning to smoke; add about one-third of beef to pot. Cook without moving pieces until well browned, 2 to 3 minutes; using tongs, turn each piece and continue cooking until second side is browned, about 5 minutes longer. Transfer browned beef to medium bowl. Repeat with additional oil and remaining beef. (If drippings in bottom of pot are very dark, add about 1/2 cup of the above-listed chicken or beef broth and scrape pan bottom with wooden spoon to loosen browned bits; pour liquid into bowl with browned beef, then proceed.)
- Add 1 T oil to the now-empty Dutch oven; reduce heat to medium-low. Add onions, 1/2 tsp. salt and tomato paste; cook, scraping bottom of pot with wooden spoon to loosen browned bits, until onions have released some moisture, about 5 minutes. Increase heat to medium and continue to cook, stirring occasionally, until onions are lightly browned, 12 to 14 minutes.
- Stir in garlic and cook until fragrant, about 30 seconds.
- Add flour and stir until onions are evenly coated and flour is lightly browned, about 2 minutes.
- Stir in broths, scraping pan bottom to loosen browned bits; stir in beer, thyme, bay and vinegar. Add browned beef with any accumulated juices. Salt and pepper to taste. Increase heat to medium-high and bring to full simmer, stirring occasionally.
- Cover partially, then place pot in oven. Cook until fork inserted into beef meets little resistance, about 2 to 2 1/2 hours.
- Discard thyme and bay. Adjust seasonings with salt and pepper to taste. Serve over buttered egg noodles or mashed potatoes. Can be cooled and refrigerated in airtight container for up to 4 days; reheat over medium-low heat.

54. Carmelized Onion Shitake Soup With Gruyere Blue Cheese Toasts Recipe

Serving: 6 | Prep: | Cook: 60mins | Ready in:

Ingredients

- Soup
- 1 Tbl olive oil
- 8 C vertically sliced yellow onion (about 2 lbs)
- 5 C sliced shitake caps (about 10 oz whole)
- 4 garlic cloves, minced
- 3 thyme sprigs
- 1/2 C dry white wine
- 1 (14 oz) can fat free, low sodium chicken broth
- 1 (14 oz) can fat free, low sodium beef broth
- 1/2 tsp salt
- 1/2 tsp pepper
- toasts

- 12, 1/2 inch thick slices french baguette, toasted
- 1/4 C (1 oz) gruyere
- 1/4 C (1 oz0 crumbled gorgonzola
- 1/2 tsp finely chopped fresh thyme or 1/4 tsp dried

Direction

- Soup
- Heat oil in a large pan over medium high
- Add onion to pan; sauté 15 mins over medium low or until tender and a deep golden brown (about 40 minutes), stirring occasionally
- Increase heat to medium
- Add mushrooms to pan; cook 10 mins. Or until tender, stirring frequently
- Increase heat to medium high
- Stir in garlic and thyme sprigs; cook 2 minutes or until most of the liquid evaporates
- Add broth to pan; bring to simmer
- Reduce heat and simmer 45 minutes
- Stir in salt and pepper and discard thyme sprigs
- Preheat broiler
- Arrange bread slices in a single layer on a baking pan
- Top each with 1 tsp. of both cheeses
- Broil 2 minutes or until cheese is melted
- Sprinkle thyme over cheese
- Ladle about 1 cup soup into each of 6 bowls; top each serving with 2 toasts

55. Carrot Onion Soup With A Toasted Cashew Garnish Recipe

Serving: 8 | Prep: | Cook: 40mins | Ready in:

Ingredients

- 2 tablespoons butter
- 1 large white onion chopped
- 5 cups chicken stock
- 2 tablespoons honey
- 1-1/2 pounds thin carrots peeled and chopped
- 2 tablespoons tomato paste
- 2 tablespoons long grain rice
- Grated zest of 1 orange
- 1 cup fresh orange juice
- 1/2 cup heavy whipping cream
- 1/2 teaspoon salt
- 1 teaspoon freshly ground black pepper
- 1/8 teaspoon freshly grated nutmeg
- 1 tablespoon brandy
- 1/4 cup freshly toasted cashews coarsely chopped

Direction

- In a 10-inch skillet melt the butter over medium heat.
- Add onion and sauté for 3 minutes.
- Transfer the sauté to a soup pot with stock, honey, carrots, tomato paste and rice.
- Bring to a boil then turn down the heat to medium low and let simmer covered for 30 minutes.
- Transfer soup to a food processor and puree with the orange zest, juice, cream, salt and pepper. Serve very hot in cups garnished with a sprinkle of the toasted cashews.

56. Chicken Onion Soup Recipe

Serving: 10 | Prep: | Cook: 10mins | Ready in:

Ingredients

- 1 Large yellow onion
- 2 tbs olive oil
- 1 roasted chicken (pick up from the store)
- 1 Large Box elbow macaroni
- 2 Boxes chicken stock (32 oz each)
- salt
- pepper

Direction

- Add olive oil to a skillet

- Rough chop whole onion, add to skillet and sauté till begin to brown
- Pour all chicken stock into a soup pot and heat on low.
- Skin roasted chicken, discard
- Tear chicken into bite size chunks, set aside.
- When stock is beginning to boil, add all macaroni, and turn heat to low
- Let cook for 10 minutes
- Add browned onion from skillet, add chicken
- Heat for 5 minutes and serve, add salt and pepper to taste.

57. Cream Of Onion Soup Recipe

Serving: 4 | Prep: | Cook: 30mins | Ready in:

Ingredients

- 2 Extra-large OR 4 medium onions
- 3 tablespoons unsalted butter
- 1 tablespoon all-purpose flour
- 1/2 teaspoon salt
- 2 cups chicken stock
- 1 cup milk
- 1/2 cup heavy cream
- 3 large egg yolks, lightly beaten
- 1 1/2 teaspoons paprika
- fresh ground pepper, to taste
- 3 drops hot red pepper sauce
- 2 tablespoons parsley, chopped

Direction

- Peel onions and slice very thin.
- In a saucepan melt the butter.
- Add onion.
- Sauté until golden, about 10 minutes.
- Add flour and salt.
- Gradually add chicken stock, stirring constantly.
- Cover and simmer, over low heat, for about 10 minutes OR until onions are very tender.
- Add milk and cream.

- Take a little hot soup and, stirring constantly, the beaten egg yolks.
- Add egg yolk mixture to the pot.
- Continue heating over low heat until fully hot but NOT boiling.
- Add paprika, pepper and pepper sauce.
- Serve hot.
- Garnish with chopped parsley, if desired.

58. Cream Of Vidalia Onion Soup Recipe

Serving: 6 | Prep: | Cook: 60mins | Ready in:

Ingredients

- 6 slices hickory bacon, thinly sliced
- 1 stick butter
- 3 lbs. sweet onions, thinly sliced (6-8 onions)
- 8 cloves garlic, chopped
- 2 cups dry white wine
- 4 cups chicken stock
- 1 bay leaf
- 1 tsp. dried thyme
- 1 cup sour cream
- salt and pepper to taste
- hot pepper sauce to taste
- 1/8 tsp. nutmeg
- croutons and chives to garnish

Direction

- In Dutch oven, cook bacon until crisp
- Remove bacon with slotted spoon to a paper towel leaving bacon grease in pan
- Add butter, onions and garlic, cover and cook over low heat, stirring until onions are tender and starting to caramelize
- Add wine, stock, bay leaf and thyme
- Bring to boil
- Reduce heat and simmer 30 minutes
- Remove bay leaf
- Puree in a food processor or blender in batches

- Season with salt, pepper, hot pepper sauce, and nutmeg
- Add sour cream and combine
- Garnish with bacon, croutons and chives
- Can be served chilled too

59. Creamy Curry Onion Soup Recipe

Serving: 4 | Prep: | Cook: 45mins | Ready in:

Ingredients

- 3 large onions, sliced*
- 1 pint of heavy cream**
- 2 tablespoons of butter *,**
- 1 tablespoon of green chiles, diced
- 1 tablespoon of curry power
- 1 tablespoon of sofrito (click here for recipe)
- 1 cup of water

Direction

- -In a saucepan melt the 2tbsp of butter on a medium heat, and add onions.
- -Sprinkle a little bit of salt to help draw moisture out of the onions.
- -Allow to cook uncovered and stirring until the onions become soft
- -Once soft, add curry powder and mix into the onions
- -Allow to cook for 1-2 minutes
- -Add remaining ingredients and bring to a gentle boil.
- -Once a gentle boil forms, turn the heat onto a low simmer
- -Allow to simmer covered for 15-20 minutes. Stir occasionally
- -Once done, season to your liking with salt, pepper, and fresh herbs

60. Creamy Onion Soup Recipe

Serving: 8 | Prep: | Cook: 120mins | Ready in:

Ingredients

- You need a full sized blender or food processor for this recipe.
- 4 large yellow or vidalia onions
- 1 large leek
- 3 cups baby bella mushrooms, sliced
- 3 stalks celery, sliced thinly and chopped
- 3 tsp fresh tarragon
- 4 cups homemade chicken or beef stock
- 4 cloves roasted garlic (not fresh, used roasted)
- 1/2 cup dry sherry (not cooking sherry, use the real thing)
- 2 cups heavy cream
- 6 tbs olive oil
- Aged white cheddar cheese, Hard parmesan cheese, or Good Guyere Cheese (any one of these will work depending on individual tastes)

Direction

- Slice onions into rings, cut into quarters.
- Use 2 tbs olive oil in large skillet, sauté all onions for 20 mins.
- Cut leek greens off, leaving some light green. Put greens aside.
- Slice into quarter lengths, rinse dirt off, add to onions
- Continue to sauté onions and leek till translucent and beginning to brown and caramelize.
- Pour dry sherry into mixture and reduce by 1/4.
- Set aside to cool slightly.
- Pour 1/2 stock and 1/4 of cream into blender
- Add all tarragon to liquid in blender
- Add 1/4 mushrooms to blender
- Add garlic to blender
- When onions are cool enough to work with, add 3/4 of leek & onion mixture into blender.
- Blend until all contents are pureed.

- In large Dutch oven add remainder of olive oil, heat to medium.
- Sauté remaining mushrooms and thinly sliced and chopped celery, until celery is translucent and mushrooms have released moisture.
- Add remaining 1/4 onion mixture to Dutch oven, stirring occasionally.
- Lower heat to simmer.
- Pour pureed mixture slowly into Dutch oven.
- Stir often.
- Simmer for 1 hour.
- Serve hot, grate one of the cheeses over the top.
- Take leek greens and rinse dirt off, then slice thin strings from the green to use as garnish on top in bowl.
- Croutons made from garlic rubbed bread can be floated on top as well.

61. Curried Pumpkin Soup With Maple Caramelized Onions Recipe

Serving: 4 | Prep: | Cook: 15mins | Ready in:

Ingredients

- olive oil
- 2 large yellow onions, thinly sliced
- 1/4 cup maple syrup
- 1 tablespoon grated fresh ginger
- 1/2 teaspoon curry powder (or more to taste)
- 1/4 teaspoon red pepper flakes
- 1 large sweet-tart apple (I use Fuji or Gala), peeled, cored and diced
- 15-ounce can unsweetened, unseasoned pumpkin (NOT pumpkin pie mix!)
- juice of 1 large orange
- 3 cups milk
- Kosher sea salt and fresh ground pepper to taste
- 8 small toasts

Direction

- In a large skillet over medium-high heat combine a couple of tablespoons of the olive oil and half the onion. Sauté until the onions are very soft and lightly browned, 5-6 minutes.
- Add the maple syrup and ginger, then reduce heat to medium-low and continue cooking, stirring often, until the onions are thick and caramelized, about 10 minutes. Set aside.
- Meanwhile, in a large soup pot over medium high, combine another couple of tablespoons of olive oil with the remaining onion, the curry powder, red pepper flakes and the apple. Sauté until the onion is tender, about 5 minutes.
- Mix in the pumpkin and orange juice, then transfer everything in the soup pot to a food processor. Add the milk and puree until smooth.
- Return the soup to the pot and return to a gentle simmer. Season with salt and pepper.
- To serve, ladle the soup into bowls, then top each serving with 2 toasts. Arrange some of the caramelized onions over the toasts.

62. Curried Pumpkin Soup With Mushrooms And Onions Recipe

Serving: 7 | Prep: | Cook: 10mins | Ready in:

Ingredients

- 1/2 pound of fresh, sliced mushrooms
- 1/2 cup chopped onion
- 2 Tbls. butter
- 2 Tbls. flour
- 1 tsp. curry powder
- 3 cups vegetable broth
- 1 (15oz.) can solid pack pumpkin
- 1 (12oz.) can evaporated milk
- 1 Tbls. honey
- 1/2 tsp. salt
- 1/4 tsp. pepper
- 1/4 tsp. ground nutmeg
- Minced chives

Direction

- In a large saucepan, sauté the mushrooms and onion in butter until tender. Stir in the flour and curry powder until blended. Gradually add the broth. Bring to a boil, cook and stir for 2 minutes or until thickened. Add the pumpkin, milk, honey, salt, pepper and nutmeg and heat through. Garnish with chives.

63. Delicate Clear Onion Soup Recipe

Serving: 4 | Prep: | Cook: 20mins | Ready in:

Ingredients

- 4 cups chicken broth
- 2 cups water
- 1 white onion
- 1/2 celery stalk, coarsely chopped
- 1/2 carrot, coarsely chopped
- salt to taste
- 1 cup vegetable oil
- 1/2 cup flour
- 4 medium mushrooms, thinly sliced
- 4 green onion, diced

Direction

- Combine chicken stock and water in sauce pot over med high heat. Slice the onion in half and coarsely chop one half and reserve the other.
- Add the coarsely chopped onion, carrot, celery and salt to sauce pot and bring to a boil. Reduce heat and simmer 20 minutes.
- While broth simmers heat veg. oil in small sauce pot over med. heat. Slice remaining onion into thin slices. Separate the slices, dip them into the milk and then into the flour. Fry until lightly browned. Drain on a paper towel.
- After soup is done simmering strain vegies out of the broth and toss them (or eat them I suppose ;) Pour the broth back into pan then leave on low heat to keep warm until ready. Garnish with fried onion, mushroom slices and green onions. Delicious!

64. English Onion Soup With Sage And Chedder Recipe

Serving: 4 | Prep: | Cook: 90mins | Ready in:

Ingredients

- Knob of butter
- fresh sage
- 6 cloves of garlic, peeled & crushed
- 5 red onions, peeled & sliced
- 3 Large white onions, peeled & sliced
- 3 shallots, peeled & Sliced
- 300g leeks, trimmed & sliced
- sea salt & ground black pepper
- 2 Litres stock
- 8 Slices of bread
- 200g Freshly grated chedder cheese
- Worcester sauce
- olive oil

Direction

- Put butter, 2 glugs olive oil, sage & garlic in a pan
- Stir, add onions, shallots & leeks
- Season with salt & pepper
- Place lid ajar, cook slowly for 50 mins, without colouring veg
- Remove lid for the last 20 mins
- When onions & leeks are silky, add stock, bring to the boil & simmer for 10-15 mins
- Preheat oven or grill, toast bread on both sides
- Check the correct seasoning of soup & serve
- Tear toasted bread over each bowl to fit like a lid
- Sprinkle with grated cheese & Worcester sauce
- Dress your reserved safe leaves with some olive oil & place on bread

- Place bowls in oven to melt cheese & serve

65. First Place Award Winning Onion Soup Recipe

Serving: 4 | Prep: | Cook: 20mins | Ready in:

Ingredients

- 2 quarts water
- 2 large sweet onions sliced
- 1 tablespoon beef base
- 1/4 teaspoon dried thyme
- 3 bay leaves
- 1/2 cup butter
- 2/3 cup flour
- 2 tablespoons worcestershire sauce
- 2/3 cup parmesan cheese plus additional for garnish
- 1 teaspoon seasoned salt
- 1 teaspoon freshly ground black pepper
- 1 cup freshly grated swiss cheese

Direction

- In large pot combine water, onions, base, thyme and bay leaves.
- Boil until onions are transparent.
- Strain onions from stock and reserve both.
- In small pot melt butter then add flour stirring until smooth and cook 2 minutes.
- Return stock to large pot and bring to boil.
- Slowly add roux to stock stirring until soup has thickened slightly.
- Add onions to pan along with Worcestershire sauce, parmesan cheese, salt and pepper.
- Preheat oven to 350.
- Pour soup into individual bowls and top with Swiss cheese and additional Parmesan.
- Set in preheated oven and cook 5 minutes then serve immediately.

66. Five Onion Soup With Garlic Croutons Recipe

Serving: 6 | Prep: | Cook: 20mins | Ready in:

Ingredients

- 1/4 cup unsalted butter
- 1 large leek, white and pale part only, chopped
- 1 onion, chopped
- 1 red onion, chopped
- 3 green onions, chopped
- 2 shallots, chopped
- 2 stalks celery, chopped
- 1 clove garlic, minced
- 1/2 cup dry sherry
- 1 (12 - ounce) russet potato, peeled and diced
- 8 cups chicken broth, (preferably homemade, or low-sodium)
- Chopped chives
- 12 (1/4 inch) baguette slices
- 1 tablespoon olive oil
- 1 clove garlic, crushed

Direction

- Melt the butter in a heavy large Dutch oven over medium-low heat. Add the leek, onion, red onion, green onion, shallot, celery and garlic. Sauté until translucent; about 8 minutes. Add the Sherry; simmer until the liquid evaporates. Add the potato and broth; simmer until the potato is very tender, about 20 minutes.
- Puree the soup in a blender (be very careful when pureeing hot liquids, hold the top on with a folded towel and do not overfill the containers; puree in batches). Season with salt and pepper.
- Meanwhile, brush the baguette slices with olive oil. Bake in a moderate (350 degree F) oven until crisp. Rub with the garlic.
- Bring the soup to a simmer, thinning with additional stock, if desired. Ladle into deep bowls; lay the crouton on top and sprinkle with chives.

- Per Serving: 333 Calories; 11g Fat; 20g Protein; 35g Carbohydrate; 3g Dietary Fiber; 21mg Cholesterol; 964mg Sodium.

67. French Onion Soup

Serving: 0 | Prep: | Cook: |Ready in:

Ingredients

- 2 lb medium onions, halved lengthwise, then thinly sliced lengthwise
- 3 sprigs fresh thyme
- 2 Turkish bay leaves or 1 California
- 3/4 teaspoon salt
- 1/2 stick (1/4 cup) unsalted butter
- 2 teaspoons all-purpose flour
- 3/4 cup dry white wine
- 4 cups reduced-sodium beef broth (32 fl oz)
- 1 1/2 cups water
- 1/2 teaspoon black pepper
- 6 (1/2-inch-thick) diagonal slices of baguette
- 1 (1/2-lb) piece Gruyère, Comte, or Emmental
- 2 tablespoons finely grated Parmigiano-Reggiano
- Special Equipment
- 6 (8- to 10-oz) flameproof soup crocks or ramekins; a cheese plane

Direction

- Cook onions, thyme, bay leaves, and salt in butter in a 4- to 5-quart heavy pot over moderate heat, uncovered, stirring frequently, until onions are very soft and deep golden brown, about 45 minutes. Add flour and cook, stirring, 1 minute. Stir in wine and cook, stirring, 2 minutes. Stir in broth, water, and pepper and simmer, uncovered, stirring occasionally, 30 minutes.
- While soup simmers, put oven rack in middle position and preheat oven to 350°F.
- Arrange bread in 1 layer on a large baking sheet and toast, turning over once, until completely dry, about 15 minutes.
- Remove croûtes from oven and preheat broiler. Put crocks in a shallow baking pan.
- Discard bay leaves and thyme from soup and divide soup among crocks, then float a croûte in each. Slice enough Gruyère (about 6 ounces total) with cheese plane to cover tops of crocks, allowing ends of cheese to hang over rims of crocks, then sprinkle with Parmigiano-Reggiano.
- Broil 4 to 5 inches from heat until cheese is melted and bubbly, 1 to 2 minutes.
- Cooks' note:
- Soups and croûtes can be made 3 days ahead (but do not add croûtes and cheese to soup); cool completely, uncovered, then chill soup, covered, and keep croûtes in an airtight container at room temperature. Reheat soup before proceeding with recipe.

68. French Onion Soup Gratinee Recipe

Serving: 0 | Prep: | Cook: |Ready in:

Ingredients

- 4 tablespoons butter
- 1 teaspoon salt
- 2 large red onions, thinly sliced
- 2 large sweet onions, thinly sliced
- 1 (48 fluid ounce) can chicken broth
- 1 (14 ounce) can beef broth
- ½ cup red wine
- 1 tablespoon Worcestershire sauce
- 2 sprigs fresh parsley
- 1 sprig fresh thyme leaves
- 1 bay leaf
- 1 tablespoon balsamic vinegar
- salt and freshly ground black pepper to taste
- 4 thick slices French or Italian bread
- 8 slices Gruyere or Swiss cheese slices, room temperature
- ½ cup shredded Asiago or mozzarella cheese, room temperature

- 4 pinches paprika

Direction

- Melt butter in a large pot over medium-high heat. Stir in salt, red onions and sweet onions. Cook 35 minutes, stirring frequently, until onions are caramelized and almost syrupy.
- Mix chicken broth, beef broth, red wine and Worcestershire sauce into pot. Bundle the parsley, thyme, and bay leaf with twine and place in pot. Simmer over medium heat for 20 minutes, stirring occasionally. Remove and discard the herbs. Reduce the heat to low, mix in vinegar and season with salt and pepper. Cover and keep over low heat to stay hot while you prepare the bread.
- Preheat oven broiler. Arrange bread slices on a baking sheet and broil 3 minutes, turning once, until well toasted on both sides. Remove from heat; do not turn off broiler.
- Arrange 4 large oven safe bowls or crocks on a rimmed baking sheet. Fill each bowl 2/3 full with hot soup. Top each bowl with 1 slice toasted bread, 2 slice Gruyere cheese and 1/4 of the Asiago or mozzarella cheese. Sprinkle a little bit of paprika over the top of each one.
- Broil 5 minutes, or until bubbly and golden brown. As it softens, the cheese will cascade over the sides of the crock and form a beautifully melted crusty seal. Serve immediately!

69. Garlicky Onion Soup Recipe

Serving: 1 | Prep: | Cook: 30mins | Ready in:

Ingredients

- 1 head of garlic
- 1 whole medium-large onion
- 1/4 cup olive oil
- Saute pan
- salt to taste
- pepper to taste
- 1 cup water
- Favorite Bowl
- Big soup spoon
- crusty bread
- Cup of hot herbal tea

Direction

- Peel every clove of the head of garlic.
- Slice the cloves of garlic thin and cut into strips.
- Peel the onion. Cut the onion in half and slice very thin.
- Heat olive oil in sauté pan.
- Lightly sauté the slivers of garlic until softer. Do not brown.
- Add onions.
- Add more olive oil if needed to keep garlic and onion covered.
- Sauté until onions become soft and translucent.
- Sprinkle with salt and pepper.
- Add water and simmer for 5-10 minutes.
- Add more water for servings if needed.
- Adjust salt and pepper to taste.
- Serve in a bowl. Eat with a big spoon and crusty bread.
- Enjoy your soup and bread with a cup of hot herbal tea.

70. Golden Onion Soup Recipe

Serving: 6 | Prep: | Cook: 2hours | Ready in:

Ingredients

- 3 Tbsp salted butter
- olive oil
- 4 large onions, thinly sliced w/sections separated
- 8 cups beef broth (or vegetable broth if you prefer)
- brown sugar
- worcestershire sauce
- fresh ground pepper

- dried marjoram
- honey
- sea salt
- ground mustard
- French bread, sliced 1 inch thick
- Grated parmesan cheese
- Finely shredded white cheese of your choice (I like swiss, but mozzarella or jack work too)
- *When I make a beef roast I put plenty of water in the crock pot and save it to use in this soup. Refrigerate overnight, then skim of fat, strain and freeze for use later

Direction

- In your soup pot melt butter into about 1 tablespoon olive oil over medium low heat. Add onions and grind a little pepper in there, probably a healthy half teaspoon or so. Stir to coat onions then cover and cook for 15 minutes, stirring occasionally.
- Remove cover, then sprinkle 2 loose tablespoons of brown sugar over top, grab your Worcestershire sauce and shake in about 1-2 teaspoons worth. Stir and cook until onions are brown and caramelized, about 10-15 minutes.
- Deglaze pot with 1 cup of the broth, scraping up the browned bits, add remaining broth.
- Pour some marjoram into the palm of your hand Rachael Ray style :), about a teaspoon or so, grind with the heel of your hand into the pot. Shake in a little ground mustard, half teaspoon or so. Add 3-4 tablespoons honey. Grind in about a teaspoon of sea salt. Stir the soup and bring to a boil.
- Reduce heat to low, cover and simmer at least one hour. After 30 minutes taste your broth and season if needed. Here is where I might add more salt, pepper, honey, Worcestershire sauce or any combination thereof.
- A little while before serving, heat up your broiler and lightly butter slices of French bread, sprinkle generously with parmesan and broil until well toasted.
- A lot of people float their bread, top with shredded cheese and then broil, it's fabulous that way and you can too. But by this time I'm dying to eat my soup so I usually just sprinkle cheese on top of the hot soup and place my bread on top of that.
- Note: you can use any bread you want...As you can see, leftover buns work in a pinch. If all you have is sliced white bread, set a few out to stale that morning, cut into cubes, toss in melted butter, sprinkle on the parmesan and make your own croutons. I've done this too, so I can tell you it is good that way!

71. Greek Onion Stew Stefado Recipe

Serving: 6 | Prep: | Cook: 120mins | Ready in:

Ingredients

- 2   lb   stew meat Trimmed 1" cubes
- 2   Tbls   olive oil
- 1   cup   water
- 1   cup   dry red wine
- 6   oz   tomato paste (1 can)
- 1   tsp   Dried oregano, Crumbled
- 1   Bay Leaf
- 2   tsp pickling spices in a tea ball or cheesecloth ball
- 1   tsp   cinnamon
- 1   tsp   sugar
- 1/2   tsp   salt
- 1/2   tsp   pepper
- 1   lb   yellow onions, 2" small or smaller
- 4   cloves garlic chopped
- 1   tbsp cornstarch mixed into 1/4 cup water (optional to thicken sauce) to be added in the last 10 minute of cooking

Direction

- In a large Dutch oven or heavy pot (at least a 6 quart), heat the Olive oil, brown the meat for a few minutes. Add the rest of the ingredients. The onions should be left hole and not cut, the

- pickling spices need to be in a tea ball or wrapped in a cheesecloth bag, the rest just added to the pot.
- Simmer on a low heat for 2 hours. Remove the Pickling spice ball and bay leaf.
- Serve in shallow bowls or large plate with roasted potatoes.
- The juices are great when soaked up with fresh French bread.

72. Krums Vidalia Onion Soup Recipe

Serving: 4 | Prep: | Cook: 45mins | Ready in:

Ingredients

- Search for "vidalia onions and beef bouillon On the Grill".

Direction

- I add two shakes of Worcestershire to Krum's recipe.
- Sprinkle parmesan cheese on top, and launch a few croutons.
- I've had French Onion Soup in some very fancy restaurants. They don't compare to this. They're usually so salty that I wonder if I can forgo being embalmed.

73. Kumera And Cumin Soup With Carmalised Onions Recipe

Serving: 6 | Prep: | Cook: 120mins | Ready in:

Ingredients

- SOUP
- 4x Medium to Big Kumera (sweet potato) white and/or orange flesh
- 1 onion
- 2 garlic cloves
- olive oil
- Pinch of nutmeg
- Pinch of white pepper
- 2 Cups of chicken stock
- 1TBSP of cumin powder, or seeds whatever you prefer
- 2 tsp of fennel seeds (optional)
- onions
- 2-3 Large onions
- 2 TBSP brown sugar
- 1 TBSP balsamic vinegar
- 2 tsp white or red wine vinegar
- water

Direction

- SOUP
- Cut onion and garlic and sauté' in soup pot, season.
- Add nutmeg, white pepper.
- Add chicken stock and cumin (and fennel seeds)
- Last add kumara (sweet potato)
- Top up with water just so everything is covered.
- Bring to boil, then simmer for at the most 2 hours.
- Whizz at the end till creamy.
- ONIONS
- Cut onions into rings and add all the ingredients. Liberally apply water as you go to get the desired caramelization!
- A deep fry pan is best, and simmer until the onions are sticky and soft.
- When soup is ready serve piping hot with onions placed on top and drizzle a bit of the sticky onion sauce over the top.
- Along with cracked pepper.

74. Lovely Healthy N Yummy Butternut Squash Soup With Caramelized Onions And Apples Recipe

Serving: 6 | Prep: | Cook: 40mins | Ready in:

Ingredients

- Lovely butternut squash Soup with caramelized onions and apples
- (Another heart-healthy recipe)
- 2 ribs of celery, chopped
- 1 carrot, peeled and chopped
- 1 teaspoon olive oil
- 4 cups butternut squash, peeled and seeded
- 3 cloves garlic, minced
- 1 tablespoon fresh oregano, chopped
- 1 quart water, more maybe needed
- salt and pepper to taste (if desired)
- 1 teaspoon curry powder (more or less to taste)
- 1 onion, large dice
- 1 Granny Smith apple, peeled and cored large dice
- Non-fat yogurt (optional)
- Sprigs fresh dill, washed (optional)
- green onions (optional)
- ~~~~~~~~~~~~~~~~~~~~~
- . In a soup pot, sauté the onion, celery and carrot in the oil over medium heat until the onion is golden, about 5 to 6 minutes.
- Add the squash and garlic cooking 5 minutes, stirring.
- Add the oregano and stock and simmer about 15 minutes or until the veggies are soft.
- ~~~~~~~~~~~~~~~~~~~
- While the soup is cooking, place a sauté pan at medium-high heat with 1/2 teaspoon of olive oil and sauté the diced onions.
- Cut the apple into a large dice and when the onions are golden, add to the pan, toss sautéing 2 to 3 minutes.
- ~~~~~~~~~~~~~~~~~~~
- Add the curry and cook 1 minute. Remove from the heat, add the dill (optional) and set aside.
- ~~~~~~~~~~~~~~~~~~~~~~~~~
- Place all of the cooked veggies (except the curried onions and apple mix) and liquid from the pot in a blender or food processor and blend until smooth. More stock may be needed to adjust consistency.
- ~~~~~~~~~~~~~~~~~~~~~~~~~
- Return to the soup pot and add the curried onion and apple. Simmer for 2 minutes. season to taste and adjust consistency. Serve hot or chilled.
- ~~~~~~~~~~~~~~~~~~~~
- Garnish with a dollop of yogurt and a sprig of fresh dill or onion tops.
- ~~~~~~~~~~~~~~~~~~~~

Direction

- Yummy and healthy!! :)

75. Mexican Red Onion Soup Recipe

Serving: 6 | Prep: | Cook: 70mins | Ready in:

Ingredients

- 3 tablespoons olive oil
- 6 large red onions thinly sliced
- 1 tablespoon granulated sugar
- 1 teaspoon dried oregano crumbled
- 3/4 teaspoon ground coriander
- 3/4 teaspoon ground cumin
- 1/4 teaspoon ground allspice
- 1/4 teaspoon ground cinnamon
- 1/2 cup red wine vinegar
- 1/3 cup orange juice
- 1-1/2 tablespoons all purpose flour
- 7 cups chicken stock
- 1/2 teaspoon salt
- 1/4 teaspoon freshly ground black pepper

Direction

- In large pot heat olive oil over low heat then add onions and cook stirring frequently 30 minutes.
- Sprinkle onions with sugar, oregano, coriander, cumin, allspice and cinnamon.
- Cook another 20 minutes stirring occasionally then stir in vinegar and orange juice.
- Cook another 5 minutes then sprinkle with flour and cook stirring constantly for 1 minute.
- Stir in stock and bring to boil over medium then lower heat and simmer covered for 20 minutes
- Stir in the salt and pepper and serve immediately.

76. Onion And Pepper Soup Recipe

Serving: 4 | Prep: | Cook: 20mins | Ready in:

Ingredients

- 1 large white onion
- 3 medium bell pepper
- 2 ounces butter
- 3 tablespoons tomato puree
- 1-1/2 pints beef stock
- 1 teaspoon salt
- 2 teaspoons freshly ground black pepper

Direction

- Chop onion finely.
- Remove pith and seeds from peppers then cut into thin strips.
- Melt butter then add onions and peppers and cook gently until soft.
- Add stock and bring to a boil.
- Add tomato puree, salt and pepper then simmer to desired consistency.
- Let soup cool then puree some of the soup using a liquidizer.
- Pour pureed soup back into pan with the rest and reheat to serve.

77. Onion Chowder Recipe

Serving: 6 | Prep: | Cook: 45mins | Ready in:

Ingredients

- 1 pound sliced bacon, chopped
- 4 large white onions, chopped
- salt
- 32 oz. container of chicken broth
- 1/4 cup flour
- 1 cup of whole milk or half and half
- 1/4 cup finely chopped chives

Direction

- In a large Dutch oven, cook the bacon over medium heat until crisp, about 12 minutes. Using a slotted spoon, transfer to paper towels to drain. Add the onions to the pot, season with salt and cook for about 10 minutes.
- Sprinkle the onions with the flour and stir for about 1 minute. Stir in the chicken broth and bring to a boil. Lower the heat and simmer for about 30 minutes.
- Stir in the milk or half and half and heat through.
- Garnish with the bacon and chives and serve.

78. Onion Ham And Cheese Chowder Recipe

Serving: 4 | Prep: | Cook: 30mins | Ready in:

Ingredients

- 2 medium potatoes cubed
- 1/2 cup boiling water
- 1 cup chopped onion
- 3 tablespoons butter
- 3 tablespoons flour
- pepper

- 3 cups milk
- 1-1/2 cups chopped ham
- 1/2 cup shredded sharp cheese

Direction

- Cook potatoes about 10 minutes.
- Drain and reserve liquid adding water to make 1 cup.
- Cook onion in butter until tender but not brown.
- Blend in flour and pepper.
- Add milk and potato water all at once.
- Cook and stir until mixture thickens and bubbles.
- Add ham and cheese.
- Stir to melt cheese.

79. Onion Rivel Soup Recipe

Serving: 6 | Prep: | Cook: 10mins | Ready in:

Ingredients

- 1/4 cup butter
- 2 cups sliced onions
- 6 cups beef broth
- 1 egg
- 3/4 cup flour
- 1/2 tsp. salt
- 1 tsp black pepper

Direction

- Melt butter and add onions. Sauté until golden brown. Add broth and bring to a boil. Meanwhile, beat egg well and add flour, salt, and pepper. Mix first with tablespoon then by rubbing dough between your fingers. (No pieces larger than a pea). Sprinkle dough pieces slowly into the boiling broth, stirring constantly, but gently. Reduce heat to medium and simmer 8 to 10 minutes. Serve immediately.

80. Onion Soup Mix Recipe

Serving: 4 | Prep: | Cook: 15mins | Ready in:

Ingredients

- 3/4 cup instant minced onion
- 4 tsp onion powder
- 1/3 cup beef-flavored bouillon powder
- 1/4 tsp celery seed, crushed
- 1/4 tsp sugar

Direction

- Mix all ingredients, and store in an airtight container.
- To make soup:
- Add 2 tablespoons mix to 1 cup boiling water. Cover and simmer for 15 minutes. This makes a stronger soup than the store-bought mix, so you might want to use less.

81. Onion Soup Recipe

Serving: 4 | Prep: | Cook: 110mins | Ready in:

Ingredients

- 2 quartered and sliced large onions
- 2 qts. of water
- 8 cubes crumbled beef bouillon
- 1 c. of heavy cream
- 1 1/2 c. of shredded colby-monterey jack cheese
- 1 tsp. of salt
- 1 tsp. of coarsely ground black pepper
- 3/4 c.of all-purpose flour
- 1/2 c. of cold water

Direction

- First you want to bring 2 qtrs. of water to a boil.
- Now stir in bouillon and cook 10 min.

- Then you will want to add in the onions to the boiling water.
- Next let this simmer over a low flame for approx. 30 min.
- Add in your salt and pepper and cook for approx. 30 more min.
- Then stir in the flour into half c. of cold water making a paste.
- Whisk this into the mixture, just be sure not to break onions.
- Let this cook for around 30 min.
- Now add in cream and cheese until the cheese is completely melted.
- Serve this soup hot!

82. Onion Soup With A British Twist Recipe

Serving: 4 | Prep: | Cook: 60mins | Ready in:

Ingredients

- 50g butter
- 1kg onions finely slice
- 1 tbsp golden caster sugar
- few sprigs fresh thyme
- 3 fresh bay leave
- 150ml cider
- 1l stock vegetable
- Topping
- 4 thick slices fresh bread
- 100g mature cheddar grated
- Large handful parsley chopped

Direction

- Heat most of the butter in a pan, then add the onions, sugar and herbs.
- Season and cook, uncovered, over a low heat, stirring occasionally, for up to 40 mins until sticky and brown.
- Pour in the cider and simmer until reduced by half. Pour in the stock, bring to the boil, and then cook for 20 mins.
- To serve, heat the grill to high. Spread the bread on both sides with the remaining butter, then toast under the grill until golden. Scatter with cheese and place back under the grill until melted. Serve the soup in bowls with a slice of the toast floating in it, scattered generously with parsley.

83. Onion Soup In English Recipe

Serving: 4 | Prep: | Cook: 60mins | Ready in:

Ingredients

- 2 tbsp. unsalted butter
- ½ tbsp. olive oil
- 3 large onions, thinly sliced
- 1 clove garlic, minced
- 1 tbsp. granulated sugar
- ¼ cup brandy
- ½ tbsp. all-purpose flour
- 2 cups beef broth, homemade or canned
- ½ cup of water
- salt, freshly ground black pepper, 1 bay leaf, ¼ tsp. thyme
- 4 (1/2-inch thick) slices French bread, toasted
- 4 oz coarsely grated gruyere cheese

Direction

- Cut the onions in long thin slices. Mince the garlic.
- Heat the butter and oil in a soup pot over moderate heat. Add the onions and garlic and cook, stirring frequently, until soft, about 30 minutes.
- Sprinkle a teaspoon of sugar and cook the onions until caramelized for 5 more minutes.
- Remove the pot from the heat and add the brandy. Return the pot to the heat and cook, stirring occasionally, until almost dry.
- Sprinkle the onions with the flour and cook, stirring, for 2-3 minutes.
- Add the broth and water. Season the soup with salt, pepper thyme. Add a bay leaf. Bring

- the soup to a boil, lower the heat, and simmer, with the cover slightly ajar, about 20 minutes.
- Preheat the broiler.
- Grate the cheese coarsely.
- Arrange 4 ovenproof crocks or deep soup bowls on a baking sheet and ladle the hot soup into them.
- Sprinkle with the grated cheese, put a piece of toasted bread on top and sprinkle some more cheese on top of it.
- Broil the soups until the cheese is melted and bubbling for 1-2 minutes. Serve immediately.
- 1 serving: 352 calories, fat - 18g, carbs – 27g, protein -12g.

84. Onion Wine Soup Recipe

Serving: 8 | Prep: | Cook: 30mins | Ready in:

Ingredients

- 1/4 cup butter
- 5 large onions (I prefer vidalia)
- 5 cups beef broth
- 1/2 cup celery leaves
- 1 large potato, sliced
- 1 cup dry white wine
- 1tbsp vinegar
- 2 tsp sugar
- 1 cup light cream
- 1 tbsp minced parsley
- salt and pepper to taste

Direction

- Melt butter in a large saucepan.
- Add chopped onions, mix well
- Add beef broth, celery leaves, and potato.
- Bring to boiling, cover and simmer for 30 min.
- Puree mixture in blender. Return to saucepan and blend in wine, vinegar, and sugar.
- Bring to boiling and simmer 5 min.
- Stir in cream, parsley, salt, and pepper.
- Heat thoroughly but do not boil.
- Serve immediately.

85. Onion And Chorizo Soup Recipe

Serving: 6 | Prep: | Cook: 20mins | Ready in:

Ingredients

- 1 large yellow onion chopped
- 1 pound chorizo
- 28 ounces canned chopped tomatoes with juice
- 4 cups chicken stock
- 1 tablespoon cumin
- 1/4 teaspoon cayenne pepper
- 15 ounce can pinto beans drained
- 15 ounce can refried beans

Direction

- Cut up chorizo into small pieces.
- Cook chorizo and onions in sauté pan for 5 minutes.
- In large pot add tomatoes and chicken broth then bring to a slow boil.
- Add cumin, cayenne, onions and meat and simmer 5 minutes.
- Add refried beans and pinto beans mixing well.
- Simmer for 15 minutes more and serve.

86. Onion And Garlic Soup Recipe

Serving: 2 | Prep: | Cook: 20mins | Ready in:

Ingredients

- 1 head of garlic
- 1 whole medium-large onion
- 1/4 cup olive oil
- Saute pan
- salt to taste
- pepper to taste

- 1 cup water
- Favorite Bowl
- Big soup spoon
- crusty bread
- Cup of hot herbal tea

Direction

- Peel every clove of the head of garlic.
- Slice the cloves of garlic thin and cut into strips.
- Peel the onion. Cut the onion in half and slice very thin.
- Heat olive oil in sauté pan.
- Lightly sauté the slivers of garlic until softer. Do not brown.
- Add onions.
- Add more olive oil if needed to keep garlic and onion covered.
- Sauté until onions become soft and translucent.
- Sprinkle with salt and pepper.
- Add water and simmer for 5-10 minutes.
- Add more water for servings if needed.
- Adjust salt and pepper to taste.
- Serve in a bowl. Eat with a big spoon and crusty bread.
- Enjoy your soup and bread with a cup of hot herbal tea.

87. Onion Soup Recipe

Serving: 4 | Prep: | Cook: 50mins | Ready in:

Ingredients

- 6 big onions (3 red-3 white)
- 1 clove garlic pressed
- 1 l water
- 2 meat cubes (for broth)
- 2 50gr butter
- 1 glas dry white whine
- 4 slices old bread (1 cm each)
- shredded cheese (any kind if old)
- pepper salt to taste

Direction

- Heat oven to 225 C
- TRIC: clean the onions and put all peelings in a pan with the water on low heat cook 20 min
- Put through a strainer and keep the beautiful brown onion "broth"
- Melt butter in a frying pan
- Slice the onions
- Sauté onion slices in the butter 30 min on low heat in closed pan till soft and done
- Add a pinch of salt after 25 min
- Add wine and cook on high till alcohol is gone
- Add onion broth till onion slices covered + 1 cm
- Add cubes
- Cook 20 min on low closed pan
- Put shredded cheese on bread slices and cook in the oven 5-10 min till cheese bubbles
- Put bread slices in 4 soup bowls and fill up with onion soup

88. Outback Steakhouse Walkabout Onion Soup Recipe

Serving: 68 | Prep: | Cook: 5mins | Ready in:

Ingredients

- 2 cups yellow sweet onions, thinly sliced
- 2 tablespoons butter
- 1 (15 ounce) can chicken broth
- 1/4 teaspoon salt
- 1/4 teaspoon fresh pepper, ground
- 2 chicken bouillon cubes
- 1/4 cup Velveeta cheese, cubes, diced (compressed in measuring cup)
- 1 1/2 - 1 3/4 cups white sauce (below)
- cheddar cheese, shredded (for garnish)
- WHITE SAUCE
- 3 tablespoons butter
- 3 tablespoons flour
- 1/4 teaspoon salt
- 1 1/2 cups whole milk

Direction

- In 2 quart sauce pan place 3 tablespoons butter and sliced onions.
- Cook at low to medium heat stirring frequently until soft and clear but not brown.
- Add chicken broth from can, chicken bouillon cubes, salt, pepper, and stir until completely heated through.
- Add white sauce and Velveeta cheese. White sauce will be thick because it has been removed from the heat. Simmer on medium low heat until the cheese is melted and all ingredients are blended, stirring constantly.
- Turn temperature to warm and let cook for additional 30 to 45 minutes.
- Serve with a garnish of shredded cheddar cheese, and a couple of slices of warm dark Russian Bread.

89. Philly Cheese Steak Onion Soup For 2 Recipe

Serving: 2 | Prep: | Cook: 30mins | Ready in:

Ingredients

- French bread-1 can (11 oz) Pillsbury refrigerated crusty French loaf --- or regular fresh french /sour dough bread
- 1/2-1 teaspoon butter .use your own taste... i use more
- 1 boneless beef rib-eye steak (1/2 lb), trimmed of fat, cut into bite-size strips
- 1/4 teaspoon salt
- Dash pepper
- 1 can (18.5 oz) Progresso vegetable Classic French onion soup or campbells French onion soup.
- 1 can (4 oz) mushroom pieces and stems, drained
- 1/2 cup shredded provolone cheese (2 oz)
- 3 tablespoons chopped green bell pepper

Direction

- Heat oven to 350°F.
- Bake French loaf as directed on can.
- Meanwhile, in 2-quart saucepan, melt butter over medium heat.
- Add beef strips; sprinkle with salt and pepper.
- Cook and stir until browned.
- Stir in soup; heat to boiling.
- Reduce heat to medium-low; simmer uncovered 20 minutes.
- Stir mushrooms into soup; cook until thoroughly heated.
- Cut 2 (1-inch-thick) diagonal slices from warm loaf; reserve remaining loaf to serve with soup.
- Set oven control to broil.
- Ladle soup into 2 (15-oz) ovenproof bowls.
- Sprinkle 2 tablespoons of the cheese onto each serving.
- Top each with bread slice.
- Sprinkle bell pepper and remaining cheese evenly over each.
- Place bowls on cookie sheet; broil 4 to 6 inches from heat 1 to 2 minutes or until cheese is bubbly and bread is toasted.
- Serve soup with remaining slices of loaf.
- 2 servings (1 3/4 cups each).ok! Pick out your favourite wine and make a great salad to go with this …….yummy………

90. Pork With Eggplants Peppers And Spring Onions Recipe

Serving: 4 | Prep: | Cook: 30mins | Ready in:

Ingredients

- 1 ¾-2 lbs pork tenderloin, sliced in 1 1/4" slices
- 2 T. Creole or cajun seasoning mixed with 6 T. flour (Wondra preferred)
- 2 Thai or smaller globe eggplants, sliced in 1 ¼" slices, top and bottom tip removed
- 2 red, yellow or orange bell peppers, sliced
- 8 spring onions, tops and bottoms removed, halved lengthwise

- 1 (28 oz) can tomatoes, completely drained and chopped
- 1- 1 1/4c. apple cider
- 1 T. crushed garlic
- 1 T. ground cumin
- 1 t. crushed red pepper
- 1 T. dried basil
- 2 T. calvados
- sugar or Splenda to taste
- salt to taste
- olive oil as needed

Direction

- Dredge pork slices in Creole flour mixture. Reserve excess mixture. In two large coverable skillet, brown eggplant slices in olive oil working in batches. Remove. In the larger of the skillets quickly sear both sides of pork slices. In the second skillet, sauté the peppers and spring onions until softened. Add to pork. Add tomatoes, garlic, cumin, red pepper flakes and basil. Cook on medium for 1 minute, stirring. Add cider, bring to a boil and reduce heat to low. Cover and cook for 12-15 minutes. Add 2 T or more of the flour mixture to thicken the sauce. If using Wondra, you can add it directly to the sauce. If using regular flour, mix with a bit of water. Cook 2-3 minutes. Add Calvados and adjust salt and sweet as desired. Cook an additional minute. Voila.

91. Potato And Onion Soup Recipe

Serving: 4 | Prep: | Cook: 40mins | Ready in:

Ingredients

- 2 big onions, chopped
- 125 ml butter or margarine (1/2 cup)
- 4 big potatoes, peeled, cut into thin slices
- 12 ml cake flour (1 tablespoon)
- 250 ml water (1 cup)
- 500 ml milk (2 cups)
- 10 ml salt (2 teaspoons)

Direction

- Fry the onions in the butter while stirring.
- Add the potatoes.
- Stir in the flour gradually until everything is golden brown.
- Stir in the water, milk and salt.
- Cook until the potatoes is soft.
- Mash.
- Serve.

92. Potato Onion Cheddar Soup Recipe

Serving: 4 | Prep: | Cook: 40mins | Ready in:

Ingredients

- 1 large onion, sliced thinly
- 1/2 teaspoon salt
- 2 tablespoons oil
- 1 large garlic, minced
- 4 large potatoes, peeled and sliced
- 2 large celery stalks, sliced
- 2 cups chicken broth
- 1/2 teaspoon pepper
- 1 cup milk
- 8 oz sharp cheddar cheese, cubed or shredded
- minced parsley

Direction

- Cook garlic, onion, celery, and potatoes in oil for 10 minutes; stir often.
- Add broth, salt and pepper.
- Boil; reduce heat and simmer for 20 minutes.
- Stir in milk; heat through; add cheese and parsley.
- Makes 4 servings.

93. Potato Onion Soup With Pesto Recipe

Serving: 0 | Prep: | Cook: 30mins | Ready in:

Ingredients

- 3 large potatoes, peeled and sliced
- 1 large onion, thinly sliced
- 2 cloves of garlic, minced
- 4 cups chicken stock, flavour with extra bouillion booster if needed. I use 'Better than Chicken Bouillion' to taste
- salt and freshly ground pepper to taste
- 1/2 cup pesto

Direction

- In a saucepan, combine the potatoes, onions, garlic and chicken stock.
- Bring to a boil, then turn the heat to low and simmer, covered, for 20 minutes, or until the potatoes and onions are tender.
- Using a stick blender, puree until smooth.
- Ladle the soup into soup bowls and swirl the pesto on top.
- Serve and enjoy!

94. Potato And Onion Soup Recipe

Serving: 6 | Prep: | Cook: 40mins | Ready in:

Ingredients

- 5 pounds potatoes
- 48 ounces chicken broth
- 1 tablespoon salt
- 1 cup chopped onions
- 1 cup chopped celery
- 3 cups half and half

Direction

- Chop up potatoes then bring broth, salt, onions, celery and potatoes to a boil.
- Reduce heat and simmer 30 minutes until potatoes are tender.
- Add half and half then warm through without boiling.
- Serve into bowls and top with crumbled bacon, chopped green onions or shredded cheese.

95. ROASTED ONION SOUP Recipe

Serving: 6 | Prep: | Cook: 60mins | Ready in:

Ingredients

- 1/4 C. fresh parmesan cheese, grated
- 3 onions, cut in half lengthwise and thinly sliced
- 1/4 C. brandy
- 1 Tbs. fresh thyme, chopped
- 1/4 tsp. freshly ground black pepper
- 1 garlic head, large, cloves separated, peeled and cut
- in half
- 4 C. chicken broth
- 2 tsp.
- olive oil
- 1/4 tsp. salt
- 3 large shallots, cut in half lengthwise and thinly sliced.

Direction

- Preheat oven to 450°
- Set oven rack at the lowest level.
- Combine onions, shallots, garlic and oil in a large shallow roasting pan.
- Roast for 20 to 25 minutes, stirring every 5 minutes, or until the onions are golden.
- Remove from oven and pour in one-fourth of the chicken stock.
- Stir liquid in the pan, scraping the bottom to loosen and dissolve any caramelized bits. (The liquid will become quite dark.)

- Transfer the onion mixture to a soup pot and add brandy, thyme and the remaining chicken stock.
- Bring to a boil; reduce heat to low and simmer, covered, for 30 minutes.
- Season with salt and pepper and top with Parmesan cheese.

96. Red Onion And Blue Cheese Soup Recipe

Serving: 8 | Prep: | Cook: 30mins | Ready in:

Ingredients

- 3 tablespoons butter
- 2 large red onions thinly sliced
- 1 tablespoon minced fresh garlic
- 1/2 cup flour
- 1 teaspoon dried oregano
- 1/2 teaspoon dried dill weed
- 2/3 cup sherry
- 6 cups beef broth
- 2 cups whipping cream
- 1 cup crumbled bleu cheese
- 1 teaspoon salt
- 1 teaspoon freshly ground black pepper

Direction

- Melt butter in large heavy pot.
- Add onions and sauté over medium heat until translucent.
- Add garlic, flour, oregano and dill weed and cook 1 minute stirring constantly.
- Mixture will have a pasty consistency.
- Add sherry and continue cooking and stirring for another minute.
- Add broth and cream and bring to boil.
- Reduce heat and whisk in cheese cooking and whisking until cheese is melted.
- Add salt and pepper then serve immediately.

97. Rich Two Onion And Garlic Soup Recipe

Serving: 1 | Prep: | Cook: 1hours | Ready in:

Ingredients

- 1/4 cup water
- 1 large, sweet onion, thinly sliced
- 1 large leek, white and green parts, thinly sliced
- 5 cloves garlic, minced
- 1/4 cup dry red wine
- 1 sprig fresh thyme
- 1 tsp honey
- 1 1/4 cups Rich roasted Veggie stock (see note) or mushroom stock
- 1 tbsp chopped fresh parsley

Direction

- Heat water in a medium saucepan over medium heat.
- Add onion and cook, stirring and adding water as necessary, for 10 minutes.
- Stir in leek and garlic and cook 2-3 minutes longer.
- Add wine and stir vigorously to dislodge the browned bits from the pot, then add broth, honey and thyme.
- Cover and cook 25 minutes.
- Remove thyme stem, stir in fresh parsley and serve.

98. Roasted Pumpkin And Onion Bisque Recipe

Serving: 6 | Prep: | Cook: 20mins | Ready in:

Ingredients

- 1 large pumpkin, skin removed, and cut into medium-sized pieces
- 1 yellow onion - chopped

- 3 cloves of garlic - mashed with the blade of a knife (do not chop)
- 1 tbsp fresh thyme - finely chopped (or use the dry packaged one found in stores)
- 2 tbsp extra virgin olive oil
- salt and freshly ground black pepper - to taste
- 3 cups vegetable stock or water
- 3 tbsp dry white wine (optional, but it's the secret holiday ingredient!:))
- 1/2 to 1 tsp cardamom powder
- 1/2 tsp fennel powder (optional to your taste)
- 1 cup heavy cream

Direction

- Preheat oven to 425°F. Toss the pumpkin, onions, garlic and thyme in olive oil so that it is evenly coated and spread the mixture onto a baking tray. Season with salt and pepper and roast for 20–30 minutes until tender, stirring once or twice. Remove from oven and transfer to a large saucepot. Add the vegetable stock, wine and cardamom powder and simmer for 10 minutes. Now remove from flame and let it cool a little.
- Puree the soup in a blender until smooth and transfer to another saucepan. When ready to serve, reheat on medium flame, bring back to a simmer, then add in the heavy cream and whisk well. Remove from heat and serve hot with a piece of your favorite bread on the side. You can even garnish with more cream or bread croutons!
- Tip: You can add more vegetables like celery and carrots. A dash of nutmeg, if you like the flavor, can also add a nice zing!

99. Roaster Onion Soup Recipe

Serving: 4 | Prep: | Cook: 30mins | Ready in:

Ingredients

- 1/4 cup fresh parmesan cheese, grated
- 3 Spanish onions, cut in half lengthwise and thinly sliced
- 1/4 cup brandy
- 1 tablespoon fresh thyme, chopped
- 1/4 teaspoon freshly ground black pepper
- 1 garlic head, large, cloves separated, peeled and cut in half
- 4 cups low-sodium chicken broth
- 2 teaspoons olive oil (preferably extra-virgin olive oil)
- 1/4 teaspoon salt, or to taste 3 large shallots, cut in half lengthwise and thinly sliced.

Direction

- Set oven rack at the lowest level; preheat to 450 degrees. Combine onions, shallots, garlic and oil in a large shallow roasting pan. Roast for 20 to 25 minutes, stirring every 5 minutes, or until the onions are golden.
- Remove from oven and pour in one-fourth of the chicken stock. Stir liquid in the pan, scraping the bottom to loosen and dissolve any caramelized bits. (The liquid will become quite dark.)
- Transfer the onion mixture to a soup pot and add brandy, thyme and the remaining chicken stock. Bring to a boil; reduce heat to low and simmer, covered, for 30 minutes.
- Season with salt and pepper and top with Parmesan cheese.

100. Rosy Onion Soup Recipe

Serving: 6 | Prep: | Cook: 45mins | Ready in:

Ingredients

- 3-4 cups onions(red or sweet, preferably), sliced very thin
- 2 cloves garlic, chopped
- 1 stick plus 1T butter(the T softened)
- 1 bottle spicy tomato juice or V8 type cocktail(about 48oz)
- 3 cups stock(beef, vegetable)

- fresh parsley, chopped
- fresh basil
- salt and pepper
- 1 loaf French bread, sliced in 6 slices
- 2 cups shredded Mozzarella, Swiss or muenster cheese

Direction

- In Dutch oven or large soup pot, cook onions and garlic in butter until tender.
- Add tomato juice, stock, salt and pepper.
- Bring to boil stirring occasionally.
- Reduce heat and simmer for about 30 minutes.
- Lightly butter both sides of all slices of bread.
- Spoon soup into oven safe bowls, top each with one slice of bread and add 1/4 cup cheese to top of bread.
- Broil about 3 minutes until cheese is melted.
- Top with parsley and serve immediately.

101. Simple Red Onion Soup Recipe

Serving: 6 | Prep: | Cook: 60mins | Ready in:

Ingredients

- 1 large Spanish red onion, chopped
- 1 pound Spanish red onions, quartered and finely sliced
- Large can of tomatoes
- 4 tbsp spanish olive oil
- 5 cloves of garlic, crushed
- 1 bouquet garni bag (or make one with a bayleaf, some sprigs of thyme and a piece of orange peel)
- 300 ml (½ pint) Spanish red wine
- 1 ltr (2 pints) vegetable stock
- salt and freshly ground black pepper

Direction

- In a big heavy-based pot, fry the chopped onion gently for 10-15 minutes, until light golden. Stir in the sliced onion well and cook on a low heat for about 20 minutes until the onions are soft.
- Meanwhile, strain the tomatoes (removing the seeds, if desired). Chop the tomatoes. Keep 250 ml (½ pint) of the juice.
- Now stir the garlic into the onions and let this cook for 2-3 minutes. Now add the bouquet garni, tomatoes and juice. Mix in the red wine and bring to the boil. Keep the soup bubbling until about half of liquid has evaporated.
- Now pour in the vegetable stock, half cover and allow to simmer gently for about half an hour. Now remove the bouquet garni and check seasoning.
- Crispy croutons and a drizzle of good quality olive oil are a perfect accompaniment to this soup.

102. Slow Roasted Onion Soup Recipe

Serving: 1012 | Prep: | Cook: 30mins | Ready in:

Ingredients

- 6 medium vidalia onions, outer layers removed
- 1/4 cup bacon drippings or olive oil
- 2 leeks, white part only, chopped
- 2 ribs celery, chopped
- 2 quarts chicken stock or canned broth, low sodium
- 1 cup sweet sherry or sweet wine
- 1 cup heavy cream
- 2 tablespoons finely chopped fresh thyme
- salt and white pepper to taste
- 1 bunch fresh chives for garnish

Direction

- Wrap each onion separately in aluminum foil and place in a 300° F oven (or in the coals of a fire or grill pit) until onions feel tender all the way through, about 1 1/2 to 2 hours.

- Heat drippings in a large pot. Add leek and celery; cook until softened but not browned. Remove onions from foil, quarter and add to pot. Add chicken stock and sherry. Simmer about 45 minutes. Stir in cream and thyme. Remove from heat.
- In batches, puree mixture in a blender until smooth. Add salt and pepper to taste. Garnish each serving with chives. Serve immediately. Makes 12 servings.

103. Smoked Eggplant Onion And Apple Soup Recipe

Serving: 8 | Prep: | Cook: 30mins | Ready in:

Ingredients

- 3 large globe eggplants
- 2 sweet onions
- 3 large sweet apples (not tart like granny Smith or Macintosh)
- 1 shallot minced
- 3 T. butter or lite butter
- 1/4 cup olive oil
- 2 T. crushed garlic
- 1 t. Garam massala (an Indian spice mixture that can be found in any Indian store or in the Asian section of most supermarkets)
- 1 t. ground cumin
- 2-4 t. hot Indian curry powder, to taste
- 1 T. dried basil
- 2 qt. chicken stock
- ¼ c. cream sherry
- 12 sour cream (lite or non-fat OK)
- salt & hot sauce to taste
- pinch of sugar to taste
- Hickory or mesquite chips for smoking

Direction

- Soak the wood chips in water for about an hour before making the fire. Prepare a wood or coal fire and add the wood chips. Rinse the eggplants; slice off the top leafy part and the bottom naval. Peel the onions Cut eggplants and onions in half and rub all sides generously with olive oil. Place eggplants directly flat side down on the grill. Put the onions on a piece of heavy duty aluminum foil to keep them together. Grill over indirect heat. Grill on both sides until the eggplants are spongy but not really soft and have nice grill marks. The onions should soften, but it not too important. You are trying to get a smoky flavour on the onions too. Remove both and chop coarsely.
- While the eggplants are grilling, sauté apples and in butter until soft. Add the garlic, basil, Garam masala, cumin and 2 t. of the curry powder. Cook over medium low heat, stirring 5 minutes. Watch that it doesn't stick. Add the chicken stock and sherry. Bring to a boil and reduce heat to simmer. Cook covered for 30 minutes. Turn off heat, add sour cream. Puree soup with a hand blender. Check the curry. Since curries are all individually blended they vary widely. You may need 1-2 t. more. Check for salt. Add a little hot sauce if needed and sugar or sweetener as needed.

104. Smoked Onion And Garlic Soup Recipe

Serving: 6 | Prep: | Cook: 90mins | Ready in:

Ingredients

- 2 cups wood chips
- cooking spray
- 6 cups thinly vertically sliced yellow onion
- 15 garlic cloves
- 1 1/2 teaspoons chopped fresh or 1/2 teaspoon dried thyme
- 2 teaspoons tomato paste
- 1/2 teaspoon freshly ground black pepper
- 1/4 cup dry sherry
- 3 (14-ounce) cans less-sodium beef broth
- 12 (1/2-ounce) slices French bread baguette, toasted

- 3/4 cup (3 ounces) shredded Gruyère cheese

Direction

- Soak wood chips in water 30 minutes; drain.
- Prepare grill for indirect grilling, heating one side to low and leaving one side with no heat. Maintain temperature at 200° to 225°.
- Place wood chips on hot coals. Place a disposable aluminum foil pan on unheated side of grill. Pour 2 cups water in pan. Place grill rack on grill. Fold a 24 x 12-inch sheet of heavy-duty foil in half crosswise to form a 12-inch square. Fold edges of foil up to form a rim. Coat foil with cooking spray. Place foil tray on a baking sheet; arrange onion and garlic on foil tray. Carefully place foil tray on grill rack over foil pan on unheated side. Close lid; cook 1 hour and 15 minutes. Carefully remove foil tray from grill; place on baking sheet.
- Heat a large Dutch oven over medium-high heat. Add onion mixture, thyme, tomato paste, and pepper; cook 1 minute, stirring constantly. Add sherry and broth; bring to a boil. Cover, reduce heat, and simmer 1 hour.
- Preheat broiler.
- Ladle about 1 cup soup into each of 6 ovenproof soup bowls. Top each serving with 2 toast slices and 2 tablespoons cheese. Broil 3 minutes or until cheese melts. Serve immediately.

105. Sweet Potato And Onion Soup Recipe

Serving: 2 | Prep: | Cook: 30mins | Ready in:

Ingredients

- 2 large onions.
- black pepper
- 1 large sweet potato.
- more black pepper
- 3 cups of water

- salt & black pepper.
- optional: more black pepper. (get the idea)
- believe it or not! THAT'S IT!

Direction

- Peel Onions and cut into 1/8ths.
- Peel sweet potato and slice into thick slices.
- Put everything into a pot and bring to a boil.
- Put the flame on low and cook for about another 30 minutes.
- Let it cool a little and blend everything together with hand blender

106. The Soup Of Many Onions Recipe

Serving: 4 | Prep: | Cook: 40mins | Ready in:

Ingredients

- 4 small red new potatoes, scrubbed and cut in quarters
- 6 cups chicken stock (use water if no stock on hand)
- 4 tbsp butter
- 2 medium yellow onions, peeled, sliced
- 1 bunch scallions, trimmed, sliced
- 3 small leeks, trimmed, sliced (be sure to wash thoroughly!)
- 4 spring onions, peeled, sliced
- 3 cloves garlic, peeled, sliced
- 2 cups half-and-half
- salt and freshly ground black pepper
- Chopped chives

Direction

- Place potatoes and chicken stock in a large pot.
- Bring to a boil over medium-high heat.
- Reduce heat to medium and simmer until potatoes are tender, about 10 minutes.
- While the potatoes are cooking, melt the butter in a large skillet over medium heat.

- Throw in all the onions and the garlic and cook about 15 minutes, or until the onions are soft.
- Be sure to stir the onions frequently so that they cook evenly without burning.
- Transfer the onions to the pot containing the potatoes and stock once the potatoes are tender.
- Simmer for 5-10 more minutes, then remove from heat.
- Dump the contents of the pot in a blender (do it batch-wise if your blender won't hold all of the mixture at once) and purée.
- Return the puréed soup to the pot and add the half-and-half.
- Season to taste with salt and pepper; serve it forth in bowls and garnish with the chopped chives.

107. Triple Onion And Potato Soup Recipe

Serving: 4 | Prep: | Cook: 30mins | Ready in:

Ingredients

- 3 tablespoons butter
- 3 cloves garlic minced
- 3 yellow onions chopped
- 1 medium tomato seeded and chopped
- 2 teaspoons chopped fresh dill
- 3 potatoes peeled and diced
- 5 cups chicken stock
- 1/4 cup cream
- 1 teaspoon salt
- 1 teaspoon freshly ground black pepper
- 1/2 cup chopped fresh chives

Direction

- Heat butter in large saucepan then cook garlic, onion and tomato for five minutes.
- Stir in dill, potatoes and stock then bring to a boil and reduce heat.
- Cover and simmer 15 minutes then in food processor purée 1/3 soup mixture with cream.
- Return to pot then reheat gently and season with salt and pepper and sprinkle with chives.

108. Tuscan Onion Soup With Shaved Parmesan Recipe

Serving: 6 | Prep: | Cook: 60mins | Ready in:

Ingredients

- 3 pounds white onions (3 or 4 large)
- 4 medium leeks
- 4 ounces pancetta, in 1 piece
- 1/4 cup extra-virgin olive oil
- 6 cups chicken stock
- 3 to 4 tablespoons balsamic vinegar
- 3/4 to 1 cup fruity red wine, such as merlot or Beaujolais
- salt and pepper, to taste
- 6 slices rustic country style bread
- 2 garlic cloves, peeled, halved
- 3 ounces parmesan cheese, in 1 chunk
- 2 tablespoons fresh parsley, chopped

Direction

- Peel the onions and cut in half lengthwise. Thinly slice crosswise. Trim the leeks and cut in half lengthwise. Slice crosswise in 1/4-inch slices, using 3 inches of pale green. Place the leeks in cold water, and rinse to remove the dirt. Drain. Reserve the onions and leeks.
- Unroll the pancetta and dice into 1/4-inch pieces. Heat the olive oil in a large soup pot over medium-high heat. Add the pancetta and cook until some of the fat has been rendered, about 5 minutes. Add the onions and leeks. Sauté for 20 minutes or until tender, stirring occasionally. Add the stock, and simmer 30 minutes. Stir the vinegar, wine, salt, and pepper into the soup. Cook until thoroughly heated.

- Toast the bread slices, and rub with the peeled garlic clove halves.
- Spoon the soup into soup bowls. Float the bread croutons in the soup. Pare 4 or 5 shavings of the cheese on top of each serving. Garnish with the chopped parsley, and serve immediately.

109. Uber Allium Soup Recipe

Serving: 4 | Prep: | Cook: 100mins | Ready in:

Ingredients

- 40 cloves garlic, peeled but left whole
- 1 medium Yukon Gold potato (6 oz or so), unpeeled & cut into chunks
- 1 large Vidalia onion, cut into wedges
- 1/2 tbsp kosher salt
- 1 tbsp black pepper
- 1/2 cup water, divided
- 3 tbsp white wine
- 2 1/2 cups vegetable broth
- 1/3 cup water
- 1/2 tsp lemon juice

Direction

- Preheat oven to 400F.
- In a Dutch oven or small, covered casserole, toss together garlic, potato, onion, salt, pepper and 1/4 cup water.
- Cover and roast 35 minutes, then add remaining 1/4 cup water. Stir and re-cover, roast 30 minutes longer.
- Transfer pot to stovetop over medium-high heat. Add wine and cook briskly, stirring well to dislodge browned bits from the bottom of the pot.
- Add broth and 1/3 cup water, bring to a boil.
- Reduce heat and simmer 10 minutes, then remove from heat.
- Puree soup using an immersion blender (or in batches with a standard blender), stir in lemon juice and re-heat gently before adjusting the seasoning and serving.

110. Vidalia Onion Soup Recipe

Serving: 6 | Prep: | Cook: 60mins | Ready in:

Ingredients

- 2 tablespoons olive oil
- 3 large vidalia onions, sliced
- 3 to 4 cloves garlic, minced
- 1/2 cup dry sherry
- 5 cups chicken broth
- 1 tablespoon fresh thyme or 1 teaspoon dried thyme leaves
- 1 bay leaf
- 1/2 teaspoon hot sauce
- 1 loaf French bread, cut diagonally into
- 1-inch slices and toasted
- 8 to 12 slices swiss cheese

Direction

- In a large stockpot, heat olive oil over medium heat on stovetop.
- Add Vidalia onions; cook, stirring occasionally, for 20 minutes.
- Add garlic; continue to cook for 10 minutes.
- When onions reach a light caramel colour, add sherry; cook until liquid has almost evaporated.
- Stir in chicken broth, thyme, bay leaf, and hot sauce.
- When mixture returns to a boil, reduce heat, cover, and let soup simmer for 15 to 20 minutes.
- Remove bay leaf.
- Preheat oven to 400°.
- Ladle soup into ovenproof bowls, arrange 1 or 2 slices bread on top, and top with 2 slices Swiss cheese.
- Place bowls on a baking sheet.
- Bake until cheese is melted and bubbly.

111. Golden Onion Soup Recipe

Serving: 2 | Prep: | Cook: 145mins | Ready in:

Ingredients

- 1/4 cup butter
- 2 thinly sliced onions
- 3/4 tsp thyme
- fresh ground pepper to taste
- 1 Tbs. flour 2 cups water
- 1/2 cup dry wine (changing wines changes flavor)
- 2 Tbs. soy sauce
- 1 Tbs. honey
- 1/4 heaping cup shredded swiss cheese

Direction

- Melt butter in a sauce pan over medium heat
- Add onions thyme and season with pepper
- Cover and lower heat to low and cook very slowly till onions are translucent, stirring occasionally, about 20-25 minutes
- Cook until they are brown and well caramelized
- Add flour to onions and stir until browned (don't burn) scraping bottom for about 5 minutes
- Add water, wine, soy sauce and honey.
- Bring to a boil and reduce heat to a very slow simmer and cook till slightly thickened, about 1 1/2 hours
- Add Swiss cheese, stir until melted and serve with crusty bread

Index

A
Apple 4,42,54
Asparagus 3,23

B
Baguette 18
Banana 3,25
Beef 3,25,26,30
Beer 3,26,30
Bread 3,8,48
Butter 3,4,27,42

C
Calvados 49
Caramel 3,4,10,29,30,35,42
Carrot 3,26,32
Cashew 3,32
Champ 3,18
Cheddar 4,49
Cheese 3,4,11,13,15,17,28,29,30,31,34,43,48,51
Chicken 3,11,32,50
Chorizo 4,46
Cognac 20,30
Cream 3,8,33,34
Crumble 26,40
Cucumber 3,27
Cumin 4,41
Curry 3,34

D
Dijon mustard 28
Dumplings 3,24

E
Egg 4,48,54
Emmental 38

F
Fat 38
French bread 5,7,8,9,12,17,19,20,22,23,25,26,27,30,40,41,45,48,53,54,57

G
Garam masala 54
Garlic 3,4,11,17,37,39,46,51,54
Gouda 10
Gratin 3,4,12,38

H
Ham 4,43
Heart 3,16
Honey 3,29

L
Lime 3,24

M
Mince 35,45
Mozzarella 10,53
Mushroom 3,29,35

N
Nut 28

O
Oil 17
Olive 17,40
Onion 1,3,4,5,6,7,8,9,11,12,13,14,15,16,17,18,19,20,21,22,23,24,25,26,27,28,29,30,31,32,33,34,35,36,37,38,39,40,41,42,43,44,45,46,47,48,49,50,51,52,53,54,55,56,57,58

P

Parmesan 3,4,5,7,13,14,17,18,19,27,28,30,37,51,52,56

Peel 33,39,47,54,55,56

Pepper 4,43,48

Pesto 4,50

Pork 4,48

Port 3,29

Potato 4,49,50,55,56

Prosciutto 3,29

Pumpkin 3,4,35,51

R

Rhubarb 3,27

S

Sage 3,36

Salt 18,22,31

Serrano ham 29

Sherry 12,37

Soup 1,3,4,5,6,7,8,9,11,12,13,14,15,16,17,18,19,20,21,22,23,24,25,26,27,28,29,30,31,32,33,34,35,36,37,38,39,41,42,43,44,45,46,47,48,49,50,51,52,53,54,55,56,57,58

Squash 4,42

Steak 4,47,48

Stew 3,4,26,30,40

Sugar 17

T

Tea 33,36

Thyme 3,14,18

Tomato 3,21

V

Vegetarian 3,22

W

Wine 3,4,5,6,18,28,46

Worcestershire sauce 8,10,26,28,38,39,40

Z

Zest 27

Conclusion

Thank you again for downloading this book!

I hope you enjoyed reading about my book!

If you enjoyed this book, please take the time to share your thoughts and post a review on Amazon. It'd be greatly appreciated!

Write me an honest review about the book – I truly value your opinion and thoughts and I will incorporate them into my next book, which is already underway.

Thank you!

If you have any questions, **feel free to contact at:** *author@limerecipes.com*

Judy Gordy

limerecipes.com

Printed in Dunstable, United Kingdom